I0202765

THROUGH
THE
VEIL

THROUGH THE VEIL

BLAKE K. HEALY

CHARISMA
HOUSE

THROUGH THE VEIL by Blake Healy
Published by Charisma House, an imprint of Charisma Media
1150 Greenwood Blvd., Lake Mary, Florida 32746

Copyright © 2026 by Blake Healy. All rights reserved.

Unless otherwise noted, all Scripture quotations are taken from the Holy Bible, New International Version®, NIV®. Copyright © 1973, 1978, 1984, 2011 by Biblica, Inc.® Used by permission of Zondervan. All rights reserved worldwide. www.zondervan.com. The "NIV" and "New International Version" are trademarks registered in the United States Patent and Trademark Office by Biblica, Inc.®

Scripture quotations marked NASB are taken from the (NASB®) New American Standard Bible®, Copyright © 1960, 1971, 1977, 1995, 2020 by The Lockman Foundation. Used by permission. All rights reserved. www.lockman.org

Scripture quotations marked NLT are taken from the *Holy Bible*, New Living Translation, copyright ©1996, 2004, 2015 by Tyndale House Foundation. Used by permission of Tyndale House Publishers, Carol Stream, Illinois 60188. All rights reserved.

While the author has made every effort to provide accurate, up-to-date source information at the time of publication, statistics and other data are constantly updated. Neither the publisher nor the author assumes any responsibility for errors or for changes that occur after publication. Further, the publisher and author do not have any control over and do not assume any responsibility for third-party websites or their content.

For more resources like this, visit MyCharismaShop.com.

Cataloging-in-Publication Data is on file with the Library of Congress.

International Standard Book Number: 978-1-63641-539-0
E-book ISBN: 978-1-63641-540-6

1 2025
Printed in the United States of America

Most Charisma Media products are available at special quantity discounts for bulk purchase for sales promotions, premiums, fund-raising, and educational needs. For details, call us at (407) 333-0600 or visit our website at charismamedia.com.

CONTENTS

FIVE GOLDEN ARROWS

I HAVE ALWAYS SEEN angels. I spent the first twelve years of my life unaware that what I was seeing was in any way unusual. I spent the following ten years learning how to make sense of the things I saw. And I have spent the rest of my life trying to express how these visions reveal the impossible beauty in God's nature.

For decades I've seen protection angels guarding us as we go about our daily routine, worship angels celebrating God's glory as we sing to Him in our churches, personal angels serving God's purpose in our lives, and many more. Though I have learned much about how to interpret these visions—sometimes metaphorical, sometimes literal, and other times a mysterious combination of the two—I've also learned enough to know that I would be wise to always consider myself a novice in this area.

My first book, *The Veil*, is about this journey. In a later section, we will address some foundational aspects of the gift of seeing in the spirit, but that is not the focus of this book. *Through the Veil* is about a problem—a problem I have bumped into a thousand times, in a thousand different ways. Though I've faced this issue more times than I can count, I have never been struck by it so profoundly or so personally as I was a few years ago.

AN UNEXPECTED EMAIL

It started late one evening when I suddenly felt the compulsion to check my email. This is an urge I rarely feel—much to the chagrin of anyone who's ever worked with me—and one I would usually ignore so close to bedtime, as late-night emails rarely contribute to a good night's sleep. Despite this I found myself opening my laptop to read a message from one of my closest friends.

In this message, which was sent to over a hundred others, he announced that he no longer considered himself a Christian and no longer believed in Jesus. Although he desired to continue his relationships with those who received the email, he said he would no longer attend our church services and had fully relinquished his faith.

I read through the rest of the text, which explained the reasoning and purpose behind his decision. Although a sheet of cold numbness ran over me, underneath I could hear my heart breaking into a dozen pieces. He had been a significant leader at our church for many years, and though I feared the consequences of this decision for him, his family, and the people he had led, the deepest pain came from the personal sense of betrayal.

He had been one of my dearest friends. We had discussed the struggles he had with his faith many times over the years. I believed I had been a safe place for him to discuss those struggles. Yet none of these conversations had prepared me for this sudden leap. It was like waking up to find an empty room in your house with nothing but a note to explain the disorienting absence of all the furniture and trappings of the life you thought you were building together.

I let the shock set in for twenty-four hours before even beginning to consider how I would respond. The only resolve I came to during this interlude was to wait longer. Partially because I knew that my friend would be inundated with a flood of responses to his message—some with wholehearted support, others with vitriolic disdain, and many more peppering the spaces in-between—and partly because I did not want the personal pain I felt from being just another among the hundred recipients of this message to poison whatever conversation we were to have. I decided to wait until the first wave of responders passed so I could refine my understanding of why this hurt so much.

Three months went by—much too long in some ways and not nearly long enough in others. Still unsure whether I was ready, I texted my friend, asking to meet for coffee, and he quickly agreed.

MEETING WITH A FRIEND

I sat in my car, waiting a few moments as I reviewed what I planned to say. I had no plans to try to argue or debate with him. While I enjoy arguing about a wide variety of subjects and get charged by spirited debate and discussion, in the current culture, argument and debate often become an exercise in rigidly stating your perspective as though it were beyond question and in demeaning the perspectives of others without a hint of consideration. I don't feel much motivation to convince others of the things I see in the spirit. I prefer to present what I've seen and let the fruit of these visions be their own defense, trusting in the discernment of those who hear them. I take the same approach to presenting and defending my faith.

Despite this I had landed on five points I wanted to express to my friend. These weren't theological pillars or apologetic arguments but were instead rooted in my deep concern and care for my friend, his family, and his future. As I reviewed them in my mind, I hoped they would be seen and received in that spirit.

Knowing I was starting to walk in mental circles, I took a deep breath, stepped out of my car, and walked into the coffee shop.

My friend was already at a table near the middle of the room. He looked the same as always. I don't know why some part of me expected him to look different. Even as I looked at him in the spirit, I found that very little had changed. I could still see the signs and markers of the anointing and calling on his life, as well as his personal angel standing

4

next to him. Every person I have ever met has what I call a personal angel: an angel that is with them every day of their life, serving God's purposes. While I have seen variation in the demeanor of these angels that may indicate how closely a person is following God's purposes, their attitude always reflects God's eternal love for all His children.

My friend's angel looked just the same as it had the hundreds of other times I had seen it. Though I thought I detected a more solemn expression on its face, I decided that could easily be me projecting my own feelings. I stopped looking in the spirit as my friend stood to greet me with a hug.

We started with a few pleasantries. Neither of us had ever been good at chitchat, especially with an elephant in the room, but we each did our best. I moved into the meat of the conversation, letting my friend know I was hurt—not just by his decision, but because, instead of calling or asking me over to his house, he had grouped me in with a hundred other disparate relationships. I expressed how I thought I had proved myself to be a safe place to process things like this and how, even if it wouldn't have changed the outcome, I would have liked the opportunity to walk through this together. I told him that, while I could empathize with the challenging position he was in, the way I received the message had felt devaluing compared with the connection we had built.

He expressed genuine remorse and apologized. This brought some measure of healing to my heart—enough to make me comfortable sharing the five points I had prepared.

I told him I had no interest in trying to convince him of anything but that each point represented things I knew I'd regret leaving unsaid. He accepted this and invited me to share what I had to say.

As I opened my mouth to speak about the first point, I started seeing in the spirit. Usually, this is something I initiate, but this time it activated instinctively.

I watched a golden arrow emerge from my mouth as I made my first point. The arrow was pure gold from end to end, and its trajectory carried it directly toward the center of my friend's forehead. As the tip of the arrow came within three inches of piercing my friend, his personal angel stepped forward and snatched the arrow from the air before it could reach its mark.

I WATCHED A GOLDEN ARROW EMERGE FROM MY MOUTH AS I MADE MY FIRST POINT. ITS TRAJECTORY CARRIED IT DIRECTLY TOWARD THE CENTER OF MY FRIEND'S FOREHEAD.

Though I am still often surprised by what I see in the spirit, I have become mostly comfortable with surprise, and I rarely react externally to what I see. This, however, caused me to stumble over my next few words. I stared at the golden arrow in the angel's hand, momentarily dumbfounded. I had enough history of seeing angels, particularly personal angels, to know that I wasn't witnessing any kind of celestial treachery, but I was so shocked that it took restraint to keep from bursting out with, "Whose side are you on?"

The angel's expression remained as calm as it had been when I walked in.

I recovered my composure as quickly as I could, unsure if my pause had lasted for seconds or fractions of a second, and I started building toward my second point. As I came to the key phrase of my next statement, I saw another golden arrow emerge from my mouth and fly toward my friend's head. The angel snatched it from the air, just as skillfully as before.

My heartbeat sped up. I felt flustered. I was still flabbergasted by what I was seeing, but I also noticed how my friend was responding to the things I was saying. His posture shifted. His expression grew more reserved. I didn't dare hope that what I had to say would immediately reverse his decision, but I had certainly hoped to leave some impact.

Feeling emotion rising in my throat, I spoke the next three points in rapid succession. Three arrows, each as golden as the first two, emerged from my mouth. This time they flew directly toward my friend's heart.

Before they could reach him, the angel stepped in front of my friend, and the three arrows sank deep into its chest. There the angel remained—two arrows in its hand, three in its chest. Not a single arrow had made it through to my friend.

The conversation came to a close. We both committed to do our best to remain connected during this process, expressed our affection for one another, and said our goodbyes.

I sat in my car and watched my friend drive away, still unsure how to feel about what had happened. Before my thoughts could cohere into anything more than a confused swirl, I turned to the passenger seat and saw the angel sitting there—two arrows in its hand, three in its chest.

The angel pulled the three arrows from its chest, took the five arrows that were now in its hand, and placed them tip-down in the cupholder between the two seats. It looked at me with pained kindness in its eyes and said, "I'm sorry, but your arrows are too dirty. You'll have to try again another time." Then it vanished, leaving the arrows sitting in the cupholder.

IN SEARCH OF ANSWERS

I've spent a long time thinking about those golden arrows. Were they messages my friend was unwilling or unable to hear? Maybe so, but they didn't bounce off him—his angel protected him from them. Were the messages theologically imperfect? This is possible, of course. I would never claim to be capable of delivering any message perfectly aligned with God's nature. Still, I believe everything I said, and those arrows looked perfectly golden from end to end. Did the personal pain I felt from my friend's decision and the way he delivered it somehow taint those golden arrows? I'm sure it could have, but I had spent three months working through that pain and expressed it as kindly and honestly as I could.

As previously mentioned, this was not the first time I had seen this problem. Why does anyone reject the message of Christ? Why do children who have grown up in church dismantle their faith later in life? Why do some people encounter the gospel and have their lives transformed, while it rolls off the back of so many others? Why do I see so much of God's goodness get rejected?

It's because they're hard-hearted and the gospel bounces off them. It's because they were introduced to a theologically unsound version of the gospel. It's because they were hurt by imperfect people and associated God with that hurt. While these answers undoubtedly contribute to this problem and may explain, in part, what happened during my conversation with my friend, they place most of the blame for the outcome on the receiver of the message. They don't answer the question asked by what I saw and what the angel said afterward: Why were my arrows too dirty?

WHY DO SOME PEOPLE ENCOUNTER THE GOSPEL AND HAVE THEIR LIVES TRANSFORMED, WHILE IT ROLLS OFF THE BACK OF SO MANY OTHERS?

This book represents the fruit of my exploration of this question. It has led me to a framework for thinking on this subject that goes much farther than I ever expected. While I wouldn't dare to suggest that this book is *the* answer to why people don't always receive the gospel, it is the answer to why *my* arrows were dirty—why what I had to give my friend did not pierce his heart. I hope that in exploring this with me, you will discover why some of the golden arrows you are called to release don't strike the mark in the hearts of those you love, and that you will be better equipped to be the champion of the gospel you are called to be.

I can only offer this message from my perspective. I am not a theologian, though I am a lifelong student of the Bible. I am not the leader of a church, though I have dedicated most of my life to serving the church. I am a man who has seen angels, demons, and other spiritual realities for forty years. I am a person who has sought to understand God's nature in every way I can. I am a life-long disciple of Jesus, and I seek to represent His nature and love for the world as much as He does, though I still fail quite often. It is from all these perspectives that I can offer you this message and explore why, sometimes, golden arrows fail to pierce through the veil.

PART I

SEEING IN THE SPIRIT

IN THIS SECTION I will outline what the gift of seeing in the spirit is, how we can understand and interpret the things that I and others see, and how we can apply them to our daily lives. Those who have read my four previous books on this subject may find some of this content familiar. If you would rather move quickly to the heart of this book's subject, feel free to skip ahead to part 2. For those who are not familiar with this gift, or would like to be refreshed on its function, this section is for you.

Scan the QR code or visit BlakeHealyBooks. com/throughtheveil/resources to watch a short video introducing the themes you'll explore in this section.

CHAPTER 1

FIRST STEPS

I SEE ANGELS, DEMONS, and other spiritual things with my eyes—not so differently from the way I'd see you if you were in the room with me. My childhood memories are littered with images of angels dancing in worship, standing sentinel near doorways, or ministering to people. They are also filled with memories of demons slinking around people arguing in the street, climbing around those struggling with addictions, or greedily hunting for some other opportunity to perpetuate destruction in the lives of whoever presented an opportunity.

I spent the first decade of my life mostly ignorant of the unusual nature of my experience. Though this may seem surprising, remember that when you are a kid, the whole world is new. Kids see things they don't understand almost every day. The angels and demons I saw everywhere I went fit into the tapestry of the world as organically as cityscapes, crowds of busy people, and plants and animals. Sure, my parents would sometimes comment on my "wild imagination" when I mentioned something spiritual, but their responses weren't that different from the way they would react to me asking whether the sun got wet when it went into the ocean, if fish could whistle, or any of the other childish observations kids make when trying to build a sense of the world.

When I was twelve years old, we started attending a church that taught about the gifts of the Spirit, especially prophecy. This gave me a grid for the things I was seeing more than ever before. After speaking with some of the church leaders, I learned about a gift they called "seeing in the spirit." This started me on the journey to learn how to make sense of the things I saw and use this gift in a way that honored God and blessed people.

THE ANGELS AND DEMONS I SAW EVERYWHERE FIT INTO THE TAPESTRY OF THE WORLD AS ORGANICALLY AS PLANTS AND ANIMALS.

At first everything went reasonably well. I saw angels in worship, who came into the room carrying great big banners dancing up and down the aisles of the church. After a few weeks of observing this, I noticed that every single time we got together and worshipped, the angels responded in a unique way. Something new and different happened every single time. I started sharing this with the worship team, and it encouraged them. It blessed them to hear that heaven was responding to the way we were worshipping God together.

Next, I started looking for what happened in the spirit while our pastor was preaching. One time I saw four or five angels with great big bolt cutters going through the crowd, cutting chains off people. As the pastor got into the meat of his message, I realized he was teaching about getting freedom in Christ. Maybe it was a little strange to see angels with bolt cutters, but the meaning seemed clear. He was talking about getting set free, and angels were cutting chains off people. I shared this with our pastor, and he was blessed by it, just as the worship team had been blessed by what I had seen.

Much of what I saw made a kind of intuitive sense. I saw an angel dancing around in worship, moving along with the rhythm, and then it stepped away once worship was over. That was clearly a worship angel, right?

I saw another angel standing near the entryway to the church, like a soldier standing at attention. It was wearing a suit of armor, weapon in hand, looking every bit like a guard. I concluded that it must be a protection angel.

When I shared what I saw with people, they were blessed. It showed how God was with us and how heaven was partnering with what we were doing. But not everything I saw made such intuitive sense.

I remember one time our pastor invited people to come to the front of the church to receive the baptism of the Holy Spirit. About thirty people lined up at the front, and our pastor went down the line, praying for each one.

As he did this, I saw an orangish, yellowish, and whitish smear of light come into the room. It was cloudy and indistinct. It moved in a way that was both liquid and solid as it swooshed along the line of people from one side to the other, drifted back along the way it had come, and flew out the window.

This had none of the clear innate meaning found in anything else I had seen, but I supposed that if I was seeing it, then I should share it. So I went and told the pastor what I had seen after the service was over. After I described what I had seen, the pastor asked me what I thought it meant. I had been hoping he would know, since I didn't have the foggiest idea. I told him this, and with polite confusion on his face, he asked me to let him know if it happened again. This left me feeling confused and embarrassed. Why had I seen that orangish cloud if I couldn't understand what it meant?

Some of what I saw made intuitive sense, and some was vague and mysterious. Some of the things I saw blessed people, while others confused them.

As previously mentioned, I regularly saw angels, but I also saw demons. I hadn't shared about the demons I saw that much. I knew it might be unpleasant for people to hear, but some part of me felt that I was neglecting an important facet of this gift by not talking about it. When I was thirteen, I decided I had avoided it for long enough.

Resolving to push past my reservations, one day after church I decided to give it a try. As the service ended and everyone meandered into conversations with one another, I looked around the room for a good candidate.

At least a dozen different demons were doing various things around the room. I was trying to decide which one would be the most helpful to address when my eyes locked on a man at the back of the church. He and I had already had at least one conversation about seeing in the spirit. I thought that might make this next conversation a little simpler.

I don't know how you operate when you're getting ready to do something you are scared to do, but for me, I either need to jump up and do it right away or spend the next six to eight months thinking about it. I bit my tongue, stood up, and marched directly to the man at the back. As I was getting closer, I realized I didn't want to just tell him that a demon was hanging around him; I wanted to have some *helpful* content, you know, some input, something that could be useful. Considering this as I approached, I looked at the demon, looked at what it was doing, and formed the presentation I thought would be most helpful.

Again, I was thirteen at this point, and the man was in his mid-fifties. I was only about five feet tall, and as I approached, the man appeared to be growing taller than an oak tree.

Biting my tongue again, I marched up to him, tapped him on the shoulder, and said, "E-e-excuse me, I couldn't help but notice that you have a demon hanging on your shoulder right there. And I think that maybe you should stop looking at pornography."

I realized immediately I had made some sort of mistake. The man's face turned pink, then red, and then edged toward a frightening shade of purple. He sputtered out half a dozen word fragments and then stomped away.

With a few decades of hindsight, it's easy to identify several errors I made with this first attempt at sharing about demons. However, even now I can remember how surprised I was at the man's reaction. I hadn't expected him to be excited, but whenever I saw a demon on or around someone, I almost never felt any sense of judgment about it. In fact, it was easy to see how that demon and what it was trying to do wasn't a part of them at all.

THE MORE I PRACTICED, THE MORE I UNDERSTOOD— ENOUGH TO BUILD A KIND OF SPIRITUAL VOCABULARY.

I thought that sharing about the demons I saw would make people feel the same way I did, but it usually made them angry, sad, or scared.

Some of the things I saw blessed people, some of them confused people, and some of them made people angry. Despite a mixed bag of successes and failures, I continued to practice, share, and see more and more.

Eventually, it got overwhelming. In a single worship service, I could see more happening in the spirit realm than I could possibly make sense of. If I tried to describe everything I saw in an hour-long meeting, it would have taken me a hundred hours. Even if I could describe it all, how would I know what to share? What was worth saying out loud? What was useful for others? What should I focus on? What mattered?

I didn't know.

To be honest, I didn't understand half the things I saw—maybe even fewer than half. But I kept looking, and over time a kind of language began to form: one vision at a time, one moment at a time. The more I practiced, the more I understood. My understanding was not perfect, but it was enough to build a kind of spiritual vocabulary.

CHAPTER 2

THE PURPOSE OF SEEING

THERE WAS ONE angel I saw every week at our church. He stood near the front entryway, just inside the sanctuary. He wore shining silver armor—not a scratch, smudge, or dent on it. Every week I saw him standing at attention, holding a weapon in his hand, and looking into the distance.

He looked like a middle-aged man with a salt-and-pepper beard, fine lines across his forehead, and a vigilant expression. Everything about him looked like a guard, a protector, a soldier. Despite the intuitive meaning behind his appearance, I found myself wondering what it really meant: What's the purpose of having a protection angel right there?

I felt comforted by his presence, but what did it really

mean? Was he standing there so he could stop demons from coming in the door? If so, then would it be a matter of that angel outmaneuvering or outfighting a demon that would determine if God's or the enemy's purpose came to fruition? If that was the case, then what would happen if a demon came through another door, a window, or a wall?

Beyond that, aren't we covered in the blood of Jesus? We're sitting in the middle of God's presence. We have the Holy Spirit inside us. Isn't that adequate protection on its own? What extra protection is provided by an angel standing at the door?

I was pondering this one day when a vision popped into my mind. It was like a short film that played on the screen of my imagination. In this vision I saw two kingdoms. A king from one kingdom sent an ambassador from his kingdom to the foreign kingdom. With this ambassador he sent a small honor guard, which was about thirty soldiers. These soldiers traveled with the king's ambassador down the road and into the foreign kingdom.

As they approached, I saw hundreds of soldiers standing along the walls of this foreign kingdom, far more than were with the ambassador. Once they went inside the foreign kingdom, even more soldiers appeared, thousands of them. At first it seemed like there wouldn't be much point in that honor guard if this foreign army decided to attack. They would overcome them instantly.

However, in seeing the vision, understanding came along with it. This wasn't just about the practical protection that this honor guard would provide along the road or even within the foreign kingdom. It was as much, if not more, about the statement being made by their presence. It was a statement the king was making about this ambassador: "My power goes with this person. This honor guard represents a greater power that resides within my kingdom." The presence of the honor guard was a statement of how the king valued his ambassador.

After this vision played across my mind, I turned back to look at the angel by the door. He looked exactly the same, but every detail about him came into clearer focus. Suddenly, the way his armor was so clean and well taken care of spoke to the value, care, and intentionality he showed not only to his assignment but to the person who had given it to him. Even his appearance of age spoke of longevity, maturity, experience, and skill. I found myself floored at the level of value and care revealed by every aspect of this angel's appearance.

The angel's presence was not just about literal protection; it was about the statement made by its presence.

Sometime later, our church hosted a twenty-four-hour worship conference. I came in late during the evening to find a hundred or so people in the sanctuary worshipping while a few musicians played acoustic instruments on the stage. I was fifteen years old, and at this point I had been growing increasingly frustrated with my gift of seeing. Some of what I saw was useful, but sometimes I didn't feel like it was useful at all. Some of what I saw had a clear and intuitive meaning, but much of it was vague and abstract. Sharing these things was often as confusing to others as it was to me, making me wonder why I was seeing them at all.

When you're fifteen, a lot in your life can feel confusing, and at this point it felt like the things I saw usually added to that confusion. I walked into the worship service and saw a greenish, bluish, and whitish smear of light oscillating back and forth in a consistent but indistinct pattern above the worship team. Though it was beautiful, I found it more frustrating than fascinating. "What is that?" I thought. "Why is it there? What is it doing? What am I supposed to do about it?"

Feeling defeated, I slumped into a chair in the middle of the room and sulked in a mixture of teenage angst and spiritual irritation. In the middle of this indolent attitude, my eyes were drawn to a woman in the front row. She was older, sitting hunched forward with her hands folded in her lap.

At the time, our church was well-known for having vivacious worship led by a talented group of musicians. Though it never would have been expressed, if you weren't raising your hands, standing, or dancing, others may have thought you were not worshipping with your whole heart. So as I looked at this woman sitting with her hands folded, my first thought was, "I guess she's not very engaged in worship."

The irony of my judging this woman's engagement in worship while I sat frustrated and disconnected didn't pierce my young mind, but I did feel a sudden sense of conviction run through me. As I did, I started looking in the spirit, and I could see straight through her. I could see her skeleton and internal organs. My eyes were quickly drawn to her heart, where, as it beat, I saw a little smear of greenish, bluish, and whitish light oscillating back and forth through the four chambers. It was an exact miniature replica of the one I saw on stage.

My eyes were drawn to the rest of the room, where I saw the exact same light in each person's heart moving the same way. Immediately, I heard the Holy Spirit say, "I'm syncing their heartbeats to Mine."

Through dozens of small moments like the two I just shared, I began to form an understanding about the purpose of seeing in the spirit. While some visions revealed specific information about people and their circumstances, gave hints about their prophetic destinies, or showed insight into their spiritual struggles, there was one unifying facet to everything I saw: It all revealed God's nature.

Again, some of the things I saw made intuitive sense, like the protection angel wearing armor and standing at the door. Others, like the smear of light oscillating over the worship team, were indistinct in their meaning. Even hearing the explanation that God was "syncing their heartbeats to Mine" made very little sense. The meaning was more poetic, mysterious.

IMMEDIATELY, I HEARD THE HOLY SPIRIT SAY, "I'M SYNCING THEIR HEARTBEATS TO MINE."

This is because some of God's nature makes intuitive sense. He relates to us as Father, teacher, and even friend. He makes Himself known to us—in the Scriptures and in daily life—in a relatable and knowable way. He is also holy, righteous, mysterious, and altogether unknowable. There is much in His nature that doesn't make intuitive sense.

CHAPTER 3

INTERPRETING WHAT WE SEE

O VER THE YEARS, people have asked me—sometimes kindly and sometimes critically—whether the gift of seeing in the spirit is really in the Bible. The exact phrase "seeing in the spirit" isn't found in Scripture, but the concept? That's a different story. In fact, it's all over the Bible. In some places it's front and center.

Books such as Isaiah, Jeremiah, Ezekiel, Joel, Zechariah, Daniel, and the Book of Revelation are full of prophetic imagery and supernatural vision. Descriptions of spiritual vision are sprinkled throughout the rest of the Bible as well.

Depending on how you measure it, nearly a third of the Bible consists of some kind of prophetic imagery. The

Bible is packed with accounts of people seeing things that reveal God's nature, His plans for the future, His perspective on the present, and much more.

I can understand why someone might be skeptical about the things I see. It is wise for us to be very thoughtful about anyone's individual experience and never weigh it more highly than the Bible. However, I do find it surprising when people say, "Seeing in the spirit is not in the Bible." It's not just *in* the Bible; it is one of the most common literary forms found within its pages. I would argue that it is one of the fundamental ways God has revealed His nature to us.

Still, I understand why some people find this unfamiliar or even uncomfortable. I had a dinner with one theology professor who explained it this way: Sometimes, when pastors are preparing to teach Scripture, they'll come across a passage full of prophetic imagery or revelatory vision. But because it's not immediately practical—or easy to explain—they might move past it in favor of something more concrete. This isn't done out of bad intent—just out of habit or preference or lack of context. He told me that in over twenty-five years of biblical education, he had sat under just forty-five minutes of teaching about angels.

It makes sense. Most of you reading this book have grown up in a post-spiritual society. We were raised in a culture where the tangible, the measurable, and the scientifically verifiable are given the greatest emphasis and value. This isn't a bad thing. I love science, and I believe it's one of the most powerful and helpful of all human inventions. However, I think we may have lost something fundamental to our nature and the nature of our relationship with God in our focus on the tangible.

Most church leaders only get about thirty or forty minutes a week to communicate something meaningful to their congregations. Naturally, they'll focus on what seems immediately helpful to the average listener. But over time that emphasis can create blind spots. We get used to seeing only part of what the Bible reveals—and miss much of the spiritual language threaded throughout its pages.

To understand spiritual vision—whether in biblical accounts, the experiences of others, or the stories I share in this book—we must learn to grapple with the visual poetry of prophetic imagery. Some of it is literal, some of it is metaphorical—most of it is an elegant and mysterious combination of the two.

SOME PROPHETIC IMAGERY IS LITERAL, SOME IS METAPHORICAL—MOST OF IT IS A MYSTERIOUS COMBINATION OF THE TWO.

The journey of learning how to interpret the things I see has been a lifelong process of carefully integrating the poetic and literary elements of these visions. While I won't even begin to suggest that I have arrived at a finite conclusion to this process, I doubt such a thing exists on this side of heaven. I've encountered dozens of moments of clarity, instances where decades of unclarity cohered into a surprisingly succinct picture. One of the most profound of these moments happened right after my first son was born.

As I mentioned in the introduction, every person I have ever met has a personal angel. These angels follow us everywhere we go.

Despite these being some of the angels I see most often, their core purpose had always eluded me. Anytime I tried to describe their function, the best I could manage was a list of seemingly unconnected tasks. They pray for us, worship alongside us, laugh when we laugh, cry when we cry, protect us, and serve God's purposes for our lives.

I started calling them personal angels for this very reason. The only comparison I could make for such a collection of tasks was the role of a personal assistant. Though this was missing something vital about their purpose, I couldn't describe quite how. I didn't truly begin to understand their purpose until my first son was born.

My wife, April, and I had been married for a little over a year. We had been talking about having children since before we were married, but on this particular day, we decided to start trying to get pregnant. The moment we agreed we were ready to start a family, an angel stepped into the room.

It was a little taller than April, with brown hair and pleasant blue eyes. It wore a nurse's uniform that looked like it belonged on the set of a World War II movie.

April had been a high-performance athlete in college and had been told she might have some trouble getting pregnant. Seeing this angel, I assumed it must have been a nurse angel or a pregnancy angel, a picture of how God wanted to bless the process of bearing children.

The angel followed April constantly for the three months we spent trying to get pregnant. It was with her on the day we got our first positive pregnancy test result and remained with her as her belly grew. The nurse angel often rubbed April's growing belly with a soft cloth, ran its fingers through her hair as she endured morning sickness, or massaged her back as the weight of our growing son strained her muscles.

I would often see a special angel show up in a season of need or during a unique time in a person's life. So I wasn't surprised that heaven sent an extra angel to help us during that season.

The nurse angel followed April all the way up to the day our son was born. It rode with us in the car while we rushed to the hospital after her water broke. It was with us all throughout her labor as my emotions oscillated between excited, terrified, elated, and helpless. And it was there in that indescribably powerful moment as April held our son, Haydon, for the first time.

After relishing the moment for as long as the medical staff allowed, I followed Haydon to the examination table while the nurses tended to April. As I stood there, staring at that messy, wrinkly, and beautiful little face, I suddenly realized the nurse angel was standing next to me. It was staring at our brand-new baby boy just as intently as I was.

"I guess she has to make sure the job is all the way done," I supposed.

The angel followed me as I escorted Haydon to another room for tests. It stood right next to the little crib as I changed his diaper for the first time. It followed Haydon, never letting more than a step or two come between them, for the rest of the day.

Later that night—after all the bustle of visiting uncles, aunts, grandparents, and friends had subsided—April lay fast asleep in the hospital bed while Haydon slept soundly in the tiny hospital crib.

The futon I was sleeping on seemed specially designed to cause lasting back problems, so despite my exhaustion, I was having a hard time falling asleep.

I kept staring at my sleeping son, feeling a love like none I had ever experienced well up in my chest with every passing second. Though it felt as if my eyes couldn't take enough of him in at once, I let my gaze repeatedly drift up to the angel as it stood on the opposite side of Haydon's crib.

I noticed that the angel was no longer in the nurse's uniform it had been wearing for the past several months; it was wearing a simple blue tunic. I looked at the angel, looked at my son, and then looked back at the angel.

"You're not a pregnancy angel or a nurse angel," I said. "You're his angel, aren't you?"

The angel met my gaze and smiled in a way that seemed to say, "Well, duh."

The realization that this angel had been following my wife this whole time, even before my son was conceived, washed over me. The question that had run through my mind a thousand times before—What is the purpose of a personal angel?—rolled over my thoughts once again. They pray for you, worship alongside you, laugh when you laugh, cry when you cry, and serve God's purposes for your life. It was a list of unconnected tasks, a mish-mash of good but disparate things. I hadn't been able to come up with one defining meaning behind everything I had seen personal angels do.

During my roiling thoughts, Haydon's angel looked at me, laughed, and said, "What's wrong with the idea that the Father would see fit to send someone whose only job is to love you every day that you are here on this earth?"

I had made the mistake that so many people do when trying to make sense of prophetic imagery. I had been thinking too literally, too rigidly, and too utilitarian. The only purpose I could see for personal angels resulted in a list of tasks, like having a hard time finding the forest amid a mass of trees. It occurred to me that if I listed the tasks associated with being a father or mother, I could have come up with a similarly disparate list of jobs—a list that, while true, would completely miss the power and beauty of what it means to be a mother or a father.

If we are to understand prophetic imagery, whether in the Bible or through the visions of others, we must not make the same mistake. We must first seek to understand what it reveals about God's nature. If we study prophetic imagery in the Bible and first try to understand how it relates to current events or predictions of the future, we will likely come to as incomplete a picture as my initial assessment that the angel following my wife was a nurse or pregnancy angel. Prophetic imagery has a lot to say about the past, present, and future. Prophetic imagery has function and utility. But if we don't learn to first interpret it by how it reveals God's nature, we will likely end up misguided.

Throughout the remainder of this book, I will share a series of things I've seen that answer the questions posed by my encounter with my friend and the five golden arrows. While I will strive to illustrate the meaning behind each as best I can, I invite you to begin shaping your own interpretative lens by this same principle. Prophetic imagery exists to reveal God's nature, who He is, how He relates to us, how we relate to Him, and therefore how we are to relate to the world. Some answers are very literal and practical, while others are poetic and mysterious, because this is His nature.

PART II
FROM EDEN TO EMPIRE

To understand why those golden arrows failed to pierce my friend during our conversation, we need to understand a principle that is woven thematically all throughout Scripture. As you will see, this principle creates a picture beautifully painted across the entire biblical narrative, yet most Christians are surprisingly unfamiliar with it—maybe because this subject is difficult to work into the typical Sunday morning message, or maybe because it doesn't seem easily applicable to our daily Christian walk. But it is essential to understand if we want to know how to partner with God in releasing His goodness through the veil.

Scan the QR code or visit BlakeHealyBooks.com/throughtheveil/resources to watch a short video introducing the themes you'll explore in this section.

CHAPTER 4

SPIRITUAL STRUCTURES

MOST OF THE time, when I talk about the things I see in the spirit, I focus on angels, demons, and movements of God's presence. But there is another category I've only occasionally mentioned in my writings: spiritual structures.

In the following chapter, we will dive into what these spiritual structures represent and the profound consequences they have on our lives and on the world. But for now, let's look at three examples of what these spiritual structures can look like.

WALLED IN BY LONELINESS

The other day I was out walking my dog in our neighborhood. It was a cold day, so I had a thick coat on and was trying to walk as fast as possible. I didn't want to be out there longer than necessary. A few houses down, I saw one of our neighbors taking his garbage cans to the curb for the next day's pickup. I see this man regularly. He's always polite and waves hello.

Whenever we have a conversation, he is quick to dive into an entertaining anecdote from his long and eventful life, sharing each humorous detail with excitement and energy. But as soon as that part of the conversation ends, he shuts down quickly—not rudely but abruptly—shuffling quickly back into his house.

Every time I look at this man's house in the spirit, I see tall walls surrounding it. They are neither thick nor towering—maybe six or seven feet high—but tall enough that most people couldn't see over them if they were physical. At the front are large gates. When I stop to talk with him, I see these gates open. But just before the conversation wraps up, I notice the gates slam shut. At that moment an awkwardness enters the interaction, and he ends the conversation and returns home.

I know a little about this man. He lives alone, and his kids visit him occasionally—maybe once or twice a year. He's a sweet man, and I enjoy our conversations, but I've always sensed a loneliness about him. It's not just because he lives alone or because his kids visit infrequently; it's something deeper—something soaked through his entire being. This loneliness, this closed-off nature, is palpable. When I look at his house in the spirit, those walls don't just represent his isolation; they limit my ability to see what's happening spiritually in his life. In my younger years, I might have been suspicious of this, but over time I've come to understand that it's not necessarily a sign of something secret or sinister. It's simply a reflection of his closed-off nature.

I could guess at the reasons why he's this way. I could try to judge whether this is a good trait or a bad one. But honestly, it has always felt neutral to me. Do I think it's generally better to be more open with people? Sure, but you probably shouldn't be completely open with everyone.

A PHALANX OF SOLDIERS

As I continued walking, I ran into a couple walking their dogs. This couple and I had some conflicts in the past. They've been upset when our dog gets loose and tries to play with one of their dogs, and they don't seem to appreciate how messy our kids sometimes leave our front lawn. We have five children, so I'll openly admit that our front lawn isn't the tidiest in our neighborhood. Having five children also means the door is left open more often than I'd like, and the dog does get too excited when there is someone to say "hello" to. But I've always felt like this couple's attitude is a bit too harsh, bordering on spite. I try not to take it personally, as it seems to be how they interact with most people, but it still stings a little. I do my best to be a good neighbor and combat this with kindness, always greeting them politely. I usually get a terse but civil response.

As they approached, I looked in the spirit and saw a phalanx of soldiers surrounding them. The soldiers had their shields locked together and spears pointed outward.

In the center of this formation was a taller figure that resembled one of the people in the couple. As my dog and I got closer, the phalanx tightened, the shields overlapped, and the spears moved in a defensive, almost provoking, manner. The tall figure in the center began gesturing like a commander giving orders. At that moment the woman pulled one of the dogs close and said something strict to it—though I couldn't hear exactly what. Sometimes their dogs try to greet mine, and I suppose she thought they were too exuberant. As usual, I waved and said, "Good morning." The response I got was a curt, almost militaristic, "Good morning."

As they passed, I noticed something else. The tall, commanding figure in the spirit wasn't just pointing outward; it was also pointing inward, gesturing at the person's body and highlighting small imperfections—like a spot of dirt or a crooked piece of clothing. It became clear to me that the same critical, stringent attitude they directed at others was also turned inward. This made me realize that their demeanor wasn't just the result of a bad attitude. Their critical attitude toward my family, whether it was fair or not, wasn't just a response to us but an expression of how they viewed themselves. It was part of a system, a culture, a way of measuring how to be "right."

SPIRITUAL SLUDGE

Further down the road, I came across another house where some parents were outside with their children. I say "with," but the parents were sitting in lawn chairs, absorbed in their phones, while the kids ran around hitting each other with toy swords. In the spirit I saw a thick, heavy slime covering everything. It was the kind of sludge you'd find in a shower that is long overdue for a good cleaning. Among this sludge were spiritual structures that made me think of leisure and comfort: a cozy-looking bench, a small swimming pool, all under a pretty little pagoda to provide comfort and shade. These spiritual structures gave the impression of the perfect place for resting and connecting as a family. It would have looked appealing if they weren't all covered in the same thick slime. What should have been inviting and pleasant instead looked neglected and unappealing.

So what exactly are these things I call *spiritual structures*? Are the walls around my first neighbor's house a manifestation of unseemly secrets or character deficits? Are they something demonic? They don't look demonic to me. Demonic structures tend to be messy and destructive and made of broken and splintered wood, while these walls are simple and orderly. When I see demonic structures, it's clear they are representative of the way demons seek to kill, steal, and destroy.

What about the phalanx of soldiers around the couple? They didn't seem demonic either. The tall figure in the center didn't look like a demon, but it also didn't seem angelic. It looked like it could be tied to some unhealthy aspects of their character or family culture. But is it demonic?

What about the thick sludge around that family? Is it demonic? If so, how could it cover something that otherwise seems good? If those structures—the bench, the pool, and the pagoda—are representative of something good, such as family connection, why would something demonic be allowed to grow on them?

TO UNDERSTAND THESE SPIRITUAL STRUCTURES, WE NEED TO EXPLORE THE BACKGROUND— THE STORY BEHIND THE STORY.

To understand what these things are and what they mean, we need to go back to the beginning—the very beginning. Many of you are familiar with the gospel as it is masterfully summarized in John 3:16: "For God so loved the world that he gave his one and only Son, that whoever believes in him shall not perish but have eternal life." It's a beautiful story—the centerpiece of the Bible. But to understand these spiritual structures, we need to explore the background—the story behind the story.

CHAPTER 5

GARDEN AND EMPIRE

THE STORY I'M about to share is most likely familiar to you. There is no way I could fit the breadth and depth of this narrative into the confines of this book. Even if I could, I would not be the best person to do so. What follows is an overview of the Bible, illustrating the relationship between garden and empire.

To accomplish the goals of this book, and to fit in the story without it completely taking over, I've compressed the narrative greatly and brushed over many details that are worth intimate study. I strongly recommend that anyone who reads this also make space to study this rich and beautiful subject, perhaps starting with the works of N. T. Wright. He has written many beautiful books, both academic and popular, that cover this subject with remarkable skill and thoroughness. I recommend *The Day the Revolution Began*, *How God Became King*, and *Surprised by Hope* as excellent starting points.

EXILES FROM A GARDEN

In the beginning God created the heavens and the earth. He filled the earth He created with every plant and animal. He planted a garden, and in that beautiful garden He placed a very special creation made in His image: humanity. He established a partnership with these people. They were to cultivate the garden, multiply, and spread it across the earth. In this garden God identified two unique trees: the tree of life and the tree of the knowledge of good and evil.

The people were forbidden to eat from the latter, but they were tricked by a serpent into eating from the tree, believing it would make them like God. This act was significant—not just because it was an act of disobedience but because of why they disobeyed. It is emblematic of a temptation we wrestle with to this very day: the desire to decide for ourselves what is good and what is evil. Because of this violation, they were exiled from the garden.

Outside the garden, life became difficult for the people who had been exiled. They had to work for food, and pain entered their lives. Their first two sons, Cain and Abel, brought sacrifices to God. When Abel's sacrifice pleased God and Cain's didn't, Cain became angry and killed his brother. God confronted Cain and sent him away, marking him so no one would harm him. Cain went on to found the first city, a human attempt to create order and structure outside God's garden.

In the ancient world, a garden was understood as a symbol of a divine kingdom—a place only God could create. Cities, on the other hand, represented humans' attempt to build their own version of a garden—their own order—which was a picture of the attempt to build a structure on their own idea of what was good and what was evil. As humanity grew, wickedness spread.

The attempt to create their own kind of justice, based on their own understanding of good and evil, produced further injustice, inviting even more wickedness. Eventually, seeing how rampant this wickedness had become, God sent a flood to start over with one family—a family He found to be righteous. But even after the flood, people tried to construct their own justice, built from their own idea of what was right and wrong. This even escalated as far as them attempting to build their own way to heaven: the Tower of Babel. God disrupted their plans by confusing their languages, scattering them across the earth.

These attempts to build structures based on the human idea of good and evil expanded and grew until they developed into empires, vast civilizations with laws and ethics of their own design—Egypt, Assyria, Babylon, and many more across the ages. These empires spread across the earth as living monuments to the human idea of justice. These empires often prided themselves on their systems of justice, creating detailed laws to demonstrate their superiority. But every human attempt at justice inevitably created injustice elsewhere. This pattern of building our own justice, our own kingdoms, goes back to the tree of the knowledge of good and evil: the desire to decide for ourselves what is right and wrong.

God, however, wasn't absent. He established a covenant with the people of Israel, calling them to partner with Him in spreading His kingdom. But Israel often strayed, turning to idols and other nations for security.

THIS PATTERN OF BUILDING OUR OWN JUSTICE GOES BACK TO THE FORBIDDEN TREE: THE DESIRE TO DECIDE FOR OURSELVES WHAT IS RIGHT AND WRONG.

Judges and prophets were sent to realign them with God's ways, but the cycle of faithfulness and rebellion continued. Even the kings of Israel—though a few led the people back toward His way—often led them astray.

The Old Testament ends with this tension: Empires rising and falling, each trying to create its own justice, and God's people struggling to remain faithful. Then, during the occupation by another great empire—Rome—Jesus arrived. He brought a completely different way of building a kingdom: one that was humble, upside down, and countercultural. While many expected the Messiah to be a conquering warrior, Jesus came to serve, to heal, and to teach that the least are the greatest in God's kingdom.

Jesus' way of perpetuating the kingdom was radically different from the empires of the world. It wasn't about domination or imposing laws; it was about love, humility, and partnership with God. Through His life Jesus displayed what it meant to perpetuate God's kingdom on earth. He didn't come merely so that we could go to heaven; He came to establish His kingdom on earth.

After His death, burial, resurrection, and ascension, Christians are left facing a similar tension and temptation to Adam and Eve's: God's kingdom or our own, the tree of life or the tree of the knowledge of good and evil. Empires still exist to this day—not just powerful nations but cultural values and movements, big and small. They are gigantic and interconnected modes of thought, forming the justification for laws, economic systems, individual actions, and much more. They inform everything from our perspective on government and history to the appropriate way to greet someone you're meeting for the first time.

It's important for us to recognize that these empires— the culmination of our thoughts, cultures, and values— are neither inherently good nor inherently evil. They are the result of the human conception of what is good and what is evil. This means that some thoughts, cultures, and values will be more aligned with God's kingdom, while others will be less aligned. But it also means that no human-made empire will ever be a perfect representation of God's kingdom. They will carry some thoughts, cultures, and values of God's kingdom while rejecting or even opposing others.

Later in this book, we will explore how human flaws misalign the construction of these empires away from God's kingdom, how demonic forces take advantage of these misalignments to push these empires further away from God's kingdom, and how we can partner with God in the perpetuation of His kingdom. For now, take a step back and survey the broader picture. Christians are exiles from a garden, living in a world full of empires built on the knowledge of good and evil and operating as ambassadors of God's kingdom on the earth.

A WIDER PERSPECTIVE

With this broader perspective and context for the gospel message, we can return to the stories I shared in the previous chapter to better understand them and see how they fit into the picture of a world full of empires. What is this wall I saw around my neighbor's house? What does the phalanx of soldiers around this couple represent? Why is there a coating of slime covering structures that should represent family connection?

These are spiritual structures—prophetic imagery representing how we've constructed our lives. They are pictures of the little empires we build in our families, in our churches, in our cities, and in our world.

These structures are neither purely good nor purely evil. They often carry elements of God's kingdom but are tainted by human imperfection. Every attempt to create justice without God inevitably creates injustice somewhere else. We're all exiles, longing for the garden we were created for but often building our own kingdoms in imitation.

The walls around my first neighbor's house represent the kingdom he has built for himself: a kingdom of isolation. It's not evil, but it's not heavenly either. It's a reflection of his life experiences and the choices he's made to protect himself. We've all built a structure in our lives that decides who has access to which parts of who we are. There is a good chance that much of this structure is godly. Healthy boundaries are part of God's kingdom. However, it's not difficult to imagine how painful experiences with cruelty, betrayal, and other forms of mistreatment may cause us to construct walls that aren't a true representation of godly boundaries.

The phalanx of soldiers around the couple represents their culture of criticism and control. It's a system they've built to navigate the world, but it's not aligned with God's justice. God's kingdom does have standards of practice; it requires that we act and live according to God's nature. But some of our beliefs about how we are to act and what standards we are to live by may be more influenced by the values we grew up with than by the character of God.

The thick sludge around the family represents the outcome of the economy of rest they've created—one that's out of balance and produces a kind of spiritual stagnation. The pagoda, the bench, and the pool all looked like the kind of structures that would be ideal for restful family connection, but the result was a kind of malaise, perpetuating a type of rot.

Before we move forward, I should point out that I don't (and you shouldn't) judge my neighbors based on these few spiritual observations. I could list ten good things I've seen around them and ten more bad things I've seen as well. I could also list at least ten things in my own family structure that are far from perfect, and I imagine you could find ten similar structures in yours.

The point is not to judge who has the most righteous structure; it's to become aware that we are constantly building and living from them. These structures are neither inherently demonic nor angelic; they are human. They're the result of our attempts to build our own justice, our own kingdoms. Recognizing this helps us see the spirit realm and the physical world as interconnected parts of God's creation and helps us see ourselves as ambassadors of His kingdom within it. It also reminds us that, while we may strive to build something good, only God's kingdom is perfect.

WHERE MIGHT HE BE INVITING YOU TO LET GO OF YOUR OWN KINGDOM AND EMBRACE HIS?

As we move forward, we'll explore how these structures are sometimes influenced by the demonic, how they're often created from our own desire to choose what is good and what is evil, and how we can align our lives more closely with God's justice and partner with Him in perpetuating His kingdom. For now, I encourage you to reflect on the structures in your own life. What have you built? How does it align with God's design? Where might He be inviting you to let go of your own kingdom and embrace His?

CHAPTER 6

EMPIRES OF THE MIND

THE TEMPTATION TO build structures based on our own understanding of what is good and what is evil is fundamental to our human experience. These structures—these empires—span the vast history of every nation that has ever existed on this planet, as well as every nation that exists today. They are so massive and complex that it can be difficult to contemplate and discern where the lines between godly structure, demonic structure, and human structure begin and end.

To make this as simple as possible—and to give us a chance to discover the underlying principles—I want to start with the smallest versions of these empires: the empires in our minds. The following are three stories of moments when I saw a snapshot of an empire built up in someone's mind, what the consequences of those empires were, and how we can learn to identify some of the empires that have been built in our own minds.

THE MOTHER

A young mother came to my wife and me for some counsel. She had two very young children who were born close together, and she was feeling completely overwhelmed.

April and I could empathize. We had our middle three kids extremely close together, and that was probably one of the most stressful times of our lives. We had a two-year-old, a one-year-old, and a newborn all at once while also taking care of a five-year-old. We understood how exhausting it was, and we wanted to help her navigate that season.

One of the biggest things April kept encouraging her to do was make room for self-care. We urged her to take breaks and to find moments of rest. April suggested that when the kids were napping, instead of rushing to clean or cross off to-do lists, she could do things that actually renewed her soul.

We encouraged her to lean on her husband more, to carve out time for outings with friends, and to find activities that restored her joy. But every time we brought up these ideas, she resisted. Even though her own needs were screaming at her, she didn't want to respond to them.

Most of the time, her internal dialogue sounded something like this: "I just want to be a good mother. I want to serve my kids. They're the most important people I'll ever have in my life. I want to give to them. Anytime

I'm away from them or doing something for myself, I feel like I'm neglecting them."

As we spoke with her, she often mentioned how much she admired her own mother. She described how safe, known, and loved her mother made her feel growing up. She desperately wanted to re-create that for her own children.

While that's a noble and beautiful desire, every time she described it, I would look in the spirit and see this great golden statue appear behind her. It was the epitome of an idealized motherly figure. She was holding a basket of food under one arm and a newborn baby under the other, looking nobly into the distance. Every time this young woman described the kind of mother she wanted to be, I watched that golden idol grow brighter.

As the weeks and months went on, her situation only got harder. All it took was a few bouts of sickness with the kids or a few bad nights of sleep for her already frayed nerves to snap completely.

At one point, far more insistently, April told her, "You don't just need rest to feel fulfilled or happy. You need rest to stay healthy—to stay alive." Even as my wife pleaded with her, the young woman physically shook her head.

During this conversation, I saw that same golden idol lean forward, whispering in her ear, insisting she had to live up to its standard.

Now I want to be clear: I don't think anything is wrong with her having such a high opinion of her mother. There's certainly nothing wrong with wanting to be the best mother you can be. However, when we overidealize a person—be they a pastor, leader, entrepreneur, or parent—we aren't trying to be the best we can be; we're trying to be as good as we imagine someone else to be. This can be a trap—especially if the idealization evolves into a form of idolization.

Whether this young mother meant to, she wasn't really serving heaven's idea of motherhood. She was serving a *feeling* she remembered having. She was serving an *idol* she had built in her mind: her idea of good and evil.

WHEN WE OVERIDEALIZE A PERSON, WE AREN'T TRYING TO BE THE BEST WE CAN BE; WE'RE TRYING TO BE AS GOOD AS WE IMAGINE SOMEONE ELSE TO BE.

If she'd taken a moment to reflect, she would have realized this idol was tormenting her with an unachievable goal and insisting she pursue it in a way that was actually harming her. It was demanding she sacrifice her own health and well-being to serve a standard she could never meet.

Thankfully, over time, this young mother did take my wife's advice. She asked her husband to watch the kids more often. She started making space for hobbies and other areas of purpose in her life.

The amazing thing was that, as she did, she didn't just look happier; she looked healthier. The idol I used to see behind her began to change. It went from a shining figure of gold to a statue of stone.

By making room in her life for things that fulfilled her and brought her peace and joy—fruits of the Spirit—she transformed that idol. It became something true, something grounded. It was no longer a tormenting standard she had to live up to. It became a genuine, healthy value: an inspired vision of the kind of mother she wanted to be, drawn from the love she had felt in her mother's home, but no longer driven by an impossible ideal.

THE STUDENT

Many years ago, a student at our school of ministry was dealing with some addiction issues. It was a cycle he had dealt with for most of his life, and no matter what he did, he just couldn't seem to get out of it. Even though the struggle had been consistent, his engagement with his church community around it was equally consistent. He'd regularly confess the outcome of his addiction to pastors and other leaders in his environment, receiving prayer and ministry each time. This cycle of repentance, ministry, and relapse continued for years.

Though his confession and repentance helped reduce how often the addiction showed up in his life for a time, it always returned, growing to the exact same level it had been before.

When I looked at this young man in the spirit, I saw a garden in the ground around him. It was a beautiful garden—full of many different types of fruiting plants. The rich soil was held in place by pieces of wood around the perimeter of the garden. Rows and rows of plants were growing, thriving, and producing good fruit, but this was only true for half the garden.

While the left side of the garden was thriving, the other half was a different story. It was derelict. The few plants growing on that side looked sickly and weak and weren't producing much or any fruit. In fact, the ones farthest to the right were completely dead—shriveled and dried up. I noticed that on the right side of this garden, the wooden structure meant to hold in the soil had rotted and broken into pieces. This caused the soil to spill out.

As he told me about the cycle of repentance and ministry regarding this addiction, I saw in my mind visions of water being poured into this garden, fertilizer being added to it, and the soil being tilled and renewed. This benefited the left side of the garden but not the right side of the garden. The water leaked out through the broken boards. Tilling the soil caused the rotted boards to break even further. It was actually contributing to the problem.

As I was seeing this, I heard the Holy Spirit say that the young man needed to see a counselor.

So I asked him, "Have you ever gone to a counselor about this issue?"

"Yes, of course," he said. "I've been to see several pastoral counselors."

"That's great, but have you ever been to a professional counselor, like a licensed counselor?"

He laughed and said, "No, no, no. I don't want to mess around with any of that psychology stuff. That stuff's no good."

I felt strongly that a professional counselor was what he needed, so I challenged him on this. I suggested that someone in a different version of this field might have some tools that weren't available to all the people he had interacted with.

He scoffed at the idea. I continued to push, but he remained resistant. He didn't want to go outside the Christian circle he was familiar with. Even though I told him professional counselors existed who were also Christians—probably Christians similar to himself—he remained steadfast in this belief. He had a structure in his mind that psychology, and anything related to it, is a man-made creation and therefore inferior to anything created by God, which was, in his mind, only found within the church.

I run into this mindset often in Christian circles: the assumption that anything coming from Christians, led by Christians, or derived from church structure is somehow inherently superior. I certainly see the importance of wanting to share the values and beliefs of someone who's going to be caring for you in such an intimate way. Sticking too rigidly to this idea is rooted in the presupposition that your church or church tradition knows all there is to know about God and that He could or would not reveal something of His nature to people outside it.

When considering this principle, I'm reminded of the story of Jesus and the centurion found in Matthew 8 and Luke 7. The centurion asks Jesus to heal his servant, and when Jesus offers to come do so, the centurion insists that he is not worthy to have Jesus step into his home. Instead, the centurion cites his experience with authority—an experience gained from living in the hierarchical military structure of the Roman Empire. Based on this, the centurion tells Jesus to just speak the word, and it will be done. Jesus then compliments the centurion for his faith, and we later find that his servant was healed.

This is why I put such a strong emphasis on these empires as not being inherently good or evil. I don't think the Roman Empire, particularly during the life of Jesus, was a good representation of God's kingdom. However, something in the structure of authority that this centurion experienced made him recognize a principle of God's kingdom that had eluded most others—so much so that Jesus was astounded by his faith.

This brings me back to the story of the young student struggling with addiction. In the Christian circles he ran in, there were specific sets of tools and beliefs about how to help someone struggling in this way. While those ways of helping were good and even essential—maybe even the most important ways of helping—their tools were not complete. They didn't know how to address the structural problems that led to this cycle of addiction.

Even though the student was repenting, even though he was asking for forgiveness, and even though he was receiving ministry, he was living under the assumption that those were the only tools by which God brought kingdom structure to his life. His view of the world had been shaped by the traditions and values of the church he grew up in. This view caused him to reject what I believe would have been one of the keys to the breakthrough he so desperately needed—just because he didn't like the box it came in.

Christians are called to be imitators of Christ, not imitators of the world, so I'm not suggesting we should copy what the world does thoughtlessly, even if it looks like it's working well. However, we must proceed with the humble understanding that we don't yet know all that God's kingdom holds and that there may be facets of His kingdom that individuals or groups in the world carry more deeply than we do, just as the centurion did.

No matter how much I pressed, this young man refused to see a psychiatrist, psychologist, or licensed counselor. Years later, he was offered a leadership position at a church, and his struggle with this addiction led him to not only lose that position but also caused a lot of pain to those who had put their trust in him. As far as I know, he still hasn't dealt with his cycle of addiction, and he still hasn't gone to a professional counselor of any kind.

THE PASTOR

The next person I want to share about was a pastor at a church I visited often. While I've muted some of the details to protect his identity, the truth is that I have seen this exact pattern at several churches I've visited. I have also seen a similar outcome at many others.

I really loved visiting this church. The worship was excellent, and the atmosphere felt alive. Their staff and the students in their ministry school were dedicated servants—always there to help, always ready to support. They were generous people, truly giving of themselves.

Even though it was a wonderful church full of wonderful people, I noticed patterns over time—patterns that, as the church continued to grow, might become harmful.

The pastor had learned a pretty strict idea of church

structure from some of his mentors. On top of that, he'd had some early experiences where people betrayed his trust or built resentment toward him because of unspoken expectations. That combination of rigid teaching and personal hurt led him to build a structure that kept a wide separation between the pastoral staff and the congregation.

Now I want to say clearly: Respecting leaders is important. Recognizing that they carry a different weight of responsibility is important. There are ways to build a culture with a healthy respect for authority. But it is treacherously easy to build a culture of superiority, even without intending to do so.

Whenever I visited, I noticed people in the congregation seemed nervous about talking to me—almost like they were sneaking a cookie out of the jar if they approached to say hello or ask a question. I don't mind chatting with people when I'm out teaching—I actually enjoy it—so I found this a little odd.

One time someone came up and began telling me a long story. It might have gone on longer than necessary, but I didn't mind, as I wasn't in a hurry. Partway through, one of the head ushers hurried over and pulled the man away mid-sentence. A moment later, the pastor came up to me, apologizing profusely.

"I'm so sorry," he said. "I won't let that happen again."

Now, there's nothing wrong with protecting a guest's time. Healthy boundaries are important. But the whole exchange felt off to me—it disrespected the person who was speaking to me in an attempt to respect me. I have a hard time seeing that as a fair exchange.

Over several years of visiting, I saw that, even though there were many people in different leadership roles, the highest tiers of leadership were almost entirely made up of the pastor's family. Authority was sometimes delegated for a while, but the next year I'd visit and find it had returned to the pastor or his family again.

Despite these issues, the church continued to grow. But as more people came, the demands on leadership also grew. Unfortunately, the pastor wasn't willing to release those areas of authority to others.

Spiritually, I could see this too. Whenever I visited, I often saw two dozen angels in the room. But they were all squeezed into tiny spaces, confined and regimented. Imagine six or seven angels crammed into a three-by-three-foot square—obviously impossible in the physical, but spiritually it represented the problem perfectly. The authority structure they had created was too restrictive—not only for the number of people they needed to serve but even for what God wanted to do in their church.

During dinner one evening, I shared this vision and challenged the pastor with what I felt was a prophetic message: They were at their carrying capacity. I explained it as an ecosystem: When there's too much of one plant or animal, the land can't support it anymore, and collapse follows.

"You have to figure out how to give authority away," I told him. "You have to empower others. If you can't do that, something will break somewhere."

Sadly, about a year later, he had an affair with someone in the church. When I spoke with him about this, he was bewildered, confused about why he had even done it. I reminded him as gently as I could that when you push a system past its capacity, it will buckle somewhere. You can't always predict where it will break—but it will break.

In his case he had chosen to put all the pressure of the church on his and his family's shoulders. This made them the most natural breaking point. Unfortunately, this structure also meant no other leaders could take the reins while they made the needed repairs in their family. The church ultimately dissolved.

INTELLECTUAL HUMILITY

When we talk about "empires of the mind," the structures we build in our heads, we are talking about internal values: the mental structures of right and wrong. The only way to be good. The only way to be OK. As Christians we want these values to be rooted in God's nature. We study the Bible to understand these principles, but you don't have to look too far to find dozens of well-intentioned Christians who have wildly different ideas of what biblical values are.

The typical response I have seen to this inconsistency between them and their fellow Christians is: "They are wrong, and we are right." It may be dressed up with kinder or more authoritative language, but it usually boils down to this. As a person who grew up in church, studied the Bible my whole life, and spent a great deal of time discussing Christianity with a broad variety of

Christians, I have come to wonder: How can we tell the difference between a value born from God's nature and a value born from our own ideas about His nature?

We'll continue to explore this concept over the course of this book, but I'd like to provide an important starting point: If we wish to follow the instruction of Romans 12:2— to not conform to the pattern of this world but to be transformed by the renewing of our mind—then we must accept that our minds need renewal. We must adopt the intellectual humility to recognize that some of what we hold dear may be more rooted in the tradition and culture we grew up in than in God's nature. Some of our values may not be fully reflective of God's character. They may, in fact, be idols to our own ideas or the ideas of our forefathers.

These ideas often aren't bad in themselves. They're usually based on good values. But when they get isolated from other facets of God's nature, or when they don't integrate the broader set of values found in Scripture, problems arise. If they become too idealistic or unrealistic, they produce an empire rather than God's kingdom.

SOME OF WHAT WE HOLD DEAR MAY BE MORE ROOTED IN THE TRADITION AND CULTURE WE GREW UP IN THAN IN GOD'S NATURE.

The first story in this chapter was about a mother. Wanting to be a good mother is a beautiful and noble goal. But sometimes we build such rigid images of what "being good" looks like that we don't allow for reality, for our own needs, or for the complexity of life. Those kinds of ideals can become idols, tempting us into destructive behaviors that undermine the very things we want to build.

In the second story, it wasn't wrong that the person valued Christian-based counseling. That is a perfectly fine value. But his real value was narrower than he realized: "I only want ministry from people who are just like me." While not identical, it was culturally and spiritually identical. The tragedy was that his cycle of addiction was rooted in something his own culture didn't know how to address. He was like a sailor with scurvy on a long voyage, suffering not because of poison but because of a missing nutrient.

With the last story about the pastor, hearing it from the outside, the mistakes might seem obvious. But when you're in the middle of it—inside the pattern, inside the value system—it's incredibly hard to see. He didn't see himself as practicing nepotism or building a culture of superiority. He thought he was entrusting responsibility to the people who'd proven themselves most reliable. He couldn't see the ways his own hurt was shaping his approach to authority or how it influenced the very structure of his church.

Even now, when I speak to him, he's in deep denial that anything about his approach led to what happened. In fact, he mostly blames God for not blessing his work.

I know these stories may feel heavy, but the point isn't to condemn. It's to encourage us to remember that we're all in the process of renewal and having our minds transformed. We're constantly invited to let God gently pull down our idols and rebuild our inner structures in ways that reflect His kingdom, His values, and His love. However, this process can't start unless we recognize that we need renewal—all of us, myself included.

P∧RT III
PRINCIPALITIES AND POWERS

IN THE PREVIOUS section, we established that we are exiles from a garden, living in a world full of empires built on the knowledge of good and evil and operating as ambassadors of God's kingdom on the earth. We discussed how these empires appear in our daily lives and how they form in our minds. Until now, we haven't explored how the demonic fits into this picture. I've been intentional about this. Many Christians give the devil more credit than he deserves, often overlooking their own responsibility for the empires they build. However, I do still think it's important for us to have a clear picture of how principalities and powers try to manipulate and influence these empires to divert further from God's design.

Scan the QR code or visit BlakeHealyBooks.com/throughtheveil/resources to watch a short video introducing the themes you'll explore in this section.

CHAPTER 7

THREE PRINCIPALITIES

OVER THE PAST few chapters, we've been focusing on the idea of empire—how our own constructions, our own value systems, and our own beliefs influence the way the spirit realm interacts with the physical realm. I've intentionally put less emphasis on the demonic and its influence, because people who are attracted to this kind of content tend to overemphasize the demonic.

This comes, unintentionally, from an overly dualistic perspective: God trying to perpetuate His kingdom and His plans on the earth and the devil trying to perpetuate his. Most Christians don't consider the devil and God equal opposites, but many do consider the devil a force to be reckoned with. This tension, in my opinion,

69

creates a lowered understanding of the power of God and an overly heightened understanding of how the enemy works. I don't expect that most people reading this book would consider the devil and God as equal opposites, but as I wrote in my book *Indestructible*, the truth is far more extreme than that.

The most common metaphor in Scripture for God and the enemy is light and darkness. Light and dark aren't equal opposites. The second a light comes on, darkness flees. Darkness is nothing but the absence of light. The ultimate solution to any form of darkness is turning on a light. Whether we're turning on the light or sitting in the darkness has a lot to do with these structures—these belief systems we've been talking about. I also don't want to create the image that no force is out there trying to convince us to keep the lights off.

THE ULTIMATE SOLUTION TO ANY FORM OF DARKNESS IS TURNING ON A LIGHT.

I want to take this opportunity to talk about three principalities. In my experience a principality is a demonic force that's trying to build influence over a given area. They represent a certain set of principles or values, usually twisted versions of godly principles. As we build structures—belief systems that align with these demonic ideas—it gives the principality power over a region. Again, while I don't like giving these things more credit than they deserve, I do think it's important to recognize how these spiritual forces try to influence us.

CERTAINTY

In *Indestructible* I wrote about how media, movies, music, novels, video games, and other forms of creative work influence us. Some of these influences are beneficial, some of them aren't beneficial, and just as often, they're nuanced. I wrote about an experience I had going to the movie theater to see a romantic comedy, where I saw a group of young girls influenced negatively by what they were seeing. In that same movie theater, I saw a married couple who were being influenced positively by what they were seeing.

Most media, in my experience, is neither fully evil nor fully good in the way it influences people. Some of it may be more or less beneficial based on our season of life, our past experiences, and our ability to "eat the meat and spit out the bones." I compared media to a diet for our mind, something we eat that can influence us. I don't think it's wrong to have a slice of cake or a cookie from time to time, but if we're only eating this or eating far too much, it'll be harmful to us. In the same way, watching a movie or listening to a song that makes us feel good but maybe doesn't have explicitly Christian themes isn't inherently harmful. I do think eating too much of one kind of thing or not being attentive to how it's influencing us can be harmful.

In *Indestructible* I talked about traditional forms of media. What I didn't talk about was social media. If movies, books, video games, and music are like a diet we ingest, then social media is a twenty-four-hour buffet coming out of a fire hose.

I've spent a lot of time over the years looking in the spirit at what happens when people are scrolling through social media. But one memory sticks with me more than any other.

I travel often to teach at churches and conferences, so I spend a lot of time in airports. Airports are amazing places to people-watch, but they're overwhelming places to look in the spirit. Usually, unless I feel prompted to do so, I don't bother looking in the spirit at airports—simply because it's so busy.

But I had been feeling drawn to investigate what kind of spiritual influence social media had on people. So I decided that on all my trips, I'd pay attention to what I saw happening in the spirit as people sat in waiting areas with their eyes glued to their screens.

In general, whenever someone engages with media—whether it's music, movies, or books—I see, for lack of a better word, material come out of it. This material adds to the structures that exist in a person's spiritual life. It's usually a slow process, like decorating a shelf or adding subtle makeup to someone's complexion—small touch-ups here and there.

Social media is different. Watching someone scroll through social media in the spirit is like watching a cement pipe burst in front of their face: A torrent of structure erupts out of it, shaping and adding to spiritual frameworks at a shocking rate.

One day, when I was sitting in an airport, I observed this very thing. I noticed a middle-aged man sitting in the next row of chairs. Over his shoulder I could see he was watching a popular video podcast. I couldn't tell exactly what it was about, but in the spirit I saw this violent rush of stone erupt from his phone, rapidly adding to a statue-like structure perched on his shoulders.

This statue had an exaggeratedly masculine figure: huge muscles and broad shoulders, flexing in an almost cartoonish stance. Over just ten minutes of watching, I saw this statue swell, growing so large that it towered over the man himself. As with many spiritual structures I see, I didn't interpret it as inherently good or bad. But it struck me how disproportionate it was. It looked awkward and heavy. If the statue were a physical thing, it would have crushed him.

The man didn't look anything like the statue. He was a little overweight, had a messy beard, and wore an unmotivated expression. I had the clear sense that this image was pressing on him, suggesting that he would be more valuable if he looked and acted in line with its image of masculinity—not just physically but internally as well.

A little later I saw someone whom I assumed to be his wife come sit down next to him. I was too far away to hear their conversation, but I could see from her posture that she was frustrated. He, in turn, looked defensive and harassed. As he turned to respond, I saw the statue turn too—its expression shifting to aggression, doubling in size, and leaning forward in an intimidating pose. The weight of it bent his shoulders. Its feet buckled under its own mass as it pressed down on him.

While I don't know whether his defensiveness was justified or whether she had a good reason to be upset with him, I could see that the structure, which had been built up, wasn't helping to produce more peace in their connection.

A few seats away, a young woman with brightly colored hair was also on her phone. Because of the angle, I couldn't see what she was viewing, but I could see what came out of the screen: Bright, multicolored streams of material spilled out into a spiraling spiritual structure.

This structure was harder to describe. It looked like an abstract art piece: part tree, part sculptured metal, part fabric, and part feathers. It was in some ways beautiful but in other ways chaotic. Branches clashed in color and texture, and the whole thing didn't seem to reflect any of the natural, organic harmony that may be implied when I describe it as a tree.

Honestly, I couldn't make much sense of it, so I turned back to my notebook to work on the sermon I was planning to give at my destination. As I pulled out my Bible and set it on the little airport table, I noticed her eyes flick down. The moment she registered what it was, I saw the spiritual structure around her react.

Every branch and element twisted toward me like angry spears or stingers. Her eyes darted from the Bible to me and back, and she gave a small but unmistakable look of disgust.

Immediately, I felt a flush of offense. I found myself thinking, "You don't know me. You don't know the kind of person I am, how I treat others, how I live out my faith. You're judging me just for having this book on the table."

Normally, I don't see much in the spirit that involves

me directly. But in that moment, I experienced an unusual exception.

As I sat there feeling defensive, I saw a structure flowing out of my own notebook and Bible, just as I had seen from their phones. Around me, my own collection of spiritual symbols formed: a cross, a stained-glass window showing someone ministering to others, and a painting of a person studying Scripture. None of these seemed bad at first. But the more I looked, the more I realized they weren't images of godliness—they were images of my idea of godliness.

They were structures I had built from what I believed was the Word of God—but in truth they were my interpretations, my preferences, and my convictions.

This made me feel deeply uncomfortable—not because any of them were necessarily wrong, but because I realized they weren't representative of God. They represented my ideas about God.

I tried to shift my focus away from myself and took in the room more broadly. Imagine going from focusing on something right in your hand to seeing the whole space.

I saw people talking, scrolling social media, and watching news on the airport TVs. All around them, these structures were growing and changing, reinforced and shaped at a blinding speed.

It was overwhelming.

So I lifted my gaze higher, trying to see above it all, and that is when I saw it. Above this sea of spiritual construction was a massive pair of hands. They were sickly blue: a color I've come to associate with demonic principalities.

The fingers were entangled in hundreds of strings—each one tied to one of the spiritual structures below. The hands moved with practiced skill, pulling, twitching, and adjusting the strings. They moved with dark intelligence—a sinister artistry. A few strings even stretched down from its fingers, wrapping around the "godly" structures that surrounded me.

Beyond the hands, I could make out a huge head. Its features were obscured by a dark blue cloth that was draped over its face like a hood.

I asked the Lord, "What is this?"

Immediately, I heard the Holy Spirit say, "This is Certainty. Sometimes called Truth. Sometimes called Justice."

I realized I was looking at a principality whose entire strategy was to manipulate people into building these rigid, personal structures of truth, justice, and certainty. It didn't care what the "truth" was. It only cared that people were certain of it.

It didn't matter whether the building blocks were good or bad—just that they were arranged in a way that locked people in, kept them sure they were right, and prevented them from listening, humbling themselves, and learning.

I didn't spend too long trying to understand the details of what this principality was trying to do. I find that getting too focused on trying to discern the strategy of the enemy tends to lead us to form our own response to the enemy rather than seeking God's response. So, instead, I asked the Lord to show me the opposite of it. Rather than speaking in clear words, I felt a warm sense of knowing rise in my chest.

If I were to put it into words, it'd sound something like this: "The godly alternative to certainty is faith."

Certainty says, "I know this. I'm right. I have the full picture."

Faith says, "I know Him, and I trust Him, even in mystery."

When I looked at my own structures, as this internal shift toward faith continued to warm my chest, I saw some of the strings disentangle themselves from my structure. As they did, I could see how many of them had been built to give me certainty, to reassure me that I was right. But that isn't what God asked for.

God hadn't called me to a relationship based on proof or facts. He called me to trust Him. Building a structure to define His nature was perilously close to the early Israelites' desire to make a golden calf. He called me to operate from the fear of the Lord. I don't think this means we're to be afraid of God. We live from the fear of the Lord when we abide in the knowledge that He is God and we are not. Faith isn't the absence of knowledge but the humility to hold knowledge lightly, recognizing that He is God and we are not. I can't fully know His mind—no one can. I can always strive to know Him more, but if I build a structure out of this, even in my own mind, I'm in danger of creating an idol.

We can recognize this principality of "certainty" in our lives when we see ourselves taking pride in our convictions, insisting that our idea of justice is the only correct one, and condemning others' beliefs without interrogating our own.

In the end, faith requires trust. It requires humility. It requires the fear of the Lord—that deep, holy awareness that He is beyond us and that we will never know everything about Him. This is part of the beauty of walking with Him.

PROFIT

Some years ago, I was invited to speak at a conference. I had already been traveling and speaking at conferences for several years, but this was by far the biggest one I had ever been invited to.

Before I share the rest of this story, I want to be clear: I love the people who hosted that conference. They're a wonderful ministry, and I saw tons of great fruit come out of that event and through many of the speakers there. For the sake of what we're exploring, I'm focusing on something negative I saw, but I don't want to throw out the good while addressing the bad.

I arrived a day early, so I got to sit through all the speakers scheduled ahead of me. They delivered excellent, well-crafted messages that fit the theme of the conference. Each of them also took time to talk about projects they were working on—to promote their books and encourage donations to the ministry.

At these types of conferences, scheduled times allow for all the guest speakers to eat dinner or lunch together, meet pastors from the region, and connect more personally. Every single one of these speakers was a joy to talk with. They were real, authentic people who had served

God for most of their lives and carried a unique message that revealed a facet of His kingdom.

As the conversations went on, we started talking shop—about how the "business" of being a traveling speaker works. Most traveling speakers write a book every one to two years and travel the conference circuit to deliver messages and promote their new releases, selling copies at events as their livelihood.

As someone who grew up a missionary's kid, I've always wrestled with the tension between spiritual things and finances. Of course, we live in a world where you need money to take care of your family, to have a home, and to buy groceries. It's necessary. Receiving finances for sharing the message I feel called to preach means I can focus more time on it. At least, that's how it's been explained to me over the years.

That night in my hotel room, I thought back over how these other speakers had carried themselves—how they worked recommendations for their books into their talks and how they were so deferential to the conference hosts—not in a false or manipulative way but in a respectful way, recognizing these hosts as the ones creating the opportunity for them to speak.

IT WAS A PRINCIPALITY I HAD SEEN MANY TIMES BEFORE. THE HOLY SPIRIT HAD CALLED THIS SPIRIT PROFIT. AND IT WAS STARING RIGHT AT ME.

The next day, all these thoughts were in my mind when I got up to speak. I felt pretty nervous. This was the biggest crowd I had ever spoken to: Several thousand people were in the venue, with even more watching online.

I stepped onto the stage, gave a brief introduction, and then opened my mouth to do a short promo for my new book at the time. But as soon as I started, I saw something in the back of the room: a dark, birdlike figure. Its broad wings covered the back wall of the room. It was a principality I had seen many times before. The Holy Spirit had called this principality Profit, and it was staring right at me.

I stumbled over my words—not just because of what I saw but because of what I felt. The second Profit entered the room, I felt this internal pressure rise in me: the desire to have more opportunities to speak at conferences, to have people read my books, and to earn more money for my family so we could have more margin, more comfort. I felt a pull to conform to the pattern I had watched in the other speakers so I would be more palatable for these kinds of events.

Whether these feelings were right or wrong, I felt genuinely repulsed by them. In that moment I stopped midsentence, dropped the book promo, and went straight into the message I had prepared.

Profit hovered there for the rest of my talk. As I got to the end of the message, I realized one of the points I planned to make would challenge the views of the people who hosted the conference. It wasn't a defiant point. It wasn't critical of anyone in particular. But it wasn't perfectly aligned with what had been said before.

The moment I realized this, I saw the principality flare

up. Dark blue fire erupted between its feathers as it stared directly at me. I felt that pull even stronger—the urgency to do this "right," to make sure I was invited back, to be more agreeable so I would have future opportunities, and to provide well for my family.

Honestly, none of those desires felt inherently wrong to me. They didn't seem rooted in pride or greed. But the way they were manipulated felt deeply wrong.

Whether it was the right choice, I pushed those feelings down and spoke the message the way I felt like I was supposed to deliver it. I could tell by some of the responses that not everyone loved what I had to say. In fact, I haven't been invited back to that conference circuit since.

Before you rise up in my defense, please recognize: This is a nuanced story that's still in process. I don't know whether the way I reacted to that principality was fully right. We can all agree it's wrong for a Christian organization to be focused excessively on profits, success, and material gain. However, with these principalities and spiritual structures, we also have to be wary of overreacting in the opposite direction. There may be those who are called to fully rejecting finances or embracing poverty for its own sake, but it's not for everyone. We're not meant to live in rebellion to principalities. We're called to live in response to God.

That night I spoke with the Holy Spirit about what I had seen, and He called it Profit. He also called it Power and Success. It's a principality that tries to create structures where we're motivated by financial gain, power, or whatever the current model of "success" happens to be.

If we want to come in the opposite spirit of this structure, we need to embrace the kingdom principle of generosity. We live in a world where money is necessary but gain for its own sake isn't a truly profitable end. We're meant to be givers, helpers, and servants who use our resources to bless others.

When it comes to the ungodly Profit, one powerful antidote is learning to act with compassion. Profit doesn't care about people. It doesn't care about the effects of our gain. If we have eyes of compassion—if we care about how others are affected by the ends we're trying to justify—we're more likely to make godly decisions.

I believe this principality is called Profit precisely because it fits so well with the ethos of our age. Ultimately, it's about power; it's about conquering; and it's about personal gain. But if we have attitudes of generosity, compassion, unity, and service to others, we're less likely to be influenced by this principality.

We also need to recognize that some aspects of our modern society—especially in the US—celebrate personal gain, success, and wealth. This isn't inherently wrong, but we have to be mindful that our ultimate call is to live in response to God and His kingdom. Sometimes, however, His kingdom stands in opposition to those values or nuances within them. The culture we grow up in influences us by default, but being continually influenced by God and His kingdom takes intentionality, patience, and humility.

PRIDE

The final principality I want to address is the one I've probably seen most often. The most recent time I saw it was during a conversation with a friend of mine: a young man who's passionate, zealous, and hungry for good ideas. He spends a lot of time on social media and follows many different voices.

One day he was telling me about a particular figure—a pretty well-known person—but I'm intentionally not naming them because doing so would unhelpfully color how we hear the story. He was talking about how brilliant this person was: how influential and how full of great ideas they were.

Because this young man had asked me to speak into his life, I mentioned a few negative things I had heard about this figure. Immediately, he got defensive. "That's not true. That's just the critics. That's just people who are jealous."

I tried again, mentioning something less obviously wrong but still questionable. I got the same response: a hard no—dismissal. He couldn't even entertain the possibility that this person was anything but great.

After the third time, as he got even more defensive, I saw a principality step out from behind him.

It looked like a handsome, middle-aged man draped in long, golden robes. His skin was golden from head to toe. Despite knowing what it was, and having seen what it did many times before, I couldn't help but think, "Wow. That thing is beautiful."

Many years ago, the first time I had seen it, the Lord said, "This one's name is Pride."

In this moment Pride was holding a small statue of the figure my friend was talking about. The statue looked just as perfect as Pride did: idealized, flawless, and shimmering with every good thing that had ever been said about that person.

As I watched, a thought struck me. I asked the Lord, "What do You have to say about this person?"

Suddenly, I saw flashes of this figure's whole life. I saw the good, I saw the bad, and I saw many things in-between. I saw their childhood and their early adulthood. I saw what shaped them into who they'd become. I saw fame and fortune descend on them—partly because of their actions and character but also because of chance, the work of others, and being in the right place at the right time.

I saw the good they had done. I saw the harm they had caused. As this vision unfolded, I saw an image of them standing behind Pride. It wasn't shiny with exaggerated perfection. It was just them: a person. Like a well-taken portrait, it was honest, detailed, and true.

I described this vision to my friend. I wasn't trying to provoke him anymore. I just shared a balanced picture of who this person was: the good and the bad together.

As I spoke, I watched the statue Pride was holding soften in his hand. It melted slightly. Pride's handsome face looked politely disappointed, but it kept its charming smile. He slipped the statue back into his robe, gave a well-mannered bow, and walked away.

I saw my friend's zeal cool from fervent idealization to a simple, gentle admiration.

As previously mentioned, I've seen this principality many times. The Holy Spirit has called it Pride but also Hero and King.

This spirit doesn't just make us proud of ourselves. Just as often it makes us elevate others; it tries to get us to build monuments in our minds, turning people into heroes, perfect icons, and unassailable role models.

When Pride has a hold, we can't see the bad in someone we admire. Or we reduce people we don't like to pure villains. It polarizes us. It replaces truth with caricature. Instead of seeing someone as a whole person made in the image of God—but not living that image perfectly—it insists on simplification: idol or demon, hero or villain, all good or all bad.

This principality is obsessed with image. It pushes us to see pastors, leaders, entertainers, politicians, even friends or family, through a perfect and unrealistic lens. Or it does the reverse—reducing them to the worst things they've done, dismissing any good. It can even shape how we see ourselves, overinflating our worth or tearing us down into self-loathing.

This isn't new. The Bible shows us how it happens over and over.

Take Gideon: He wins a miraculous victory, but after he dies, the ephod he made becomes an idol people worship. The Bible doesn't shy away from sharing that part of the story. Take David: We read the psalms he wrote and see him called "a man after God's own heart," but we also read of his acts of betrayal, adultery, and murder. The Bible insists on telling the whole story. Often when I preach about David's failures, I feel the room grow tense. People want heroes to stay heroes.

That's Pride at work.

The antidote to this spirit is humility: a recognition that our value doesn't come from our own greatness but from God's. It's about service, not elevation. Jesus said the greatest in the kingdom is the servant of all. It also means practicing an integrated perspective of us and others, recognizing that everyone has both goodness and brokenness. When we fail to see that, we set ourselves up for disappointment and disillusionment.

Look at what happens whenever a public Christian figure has a public failure. The temptation is to swing from glorification to vilification. Both extremes are often rooted in the ups and downs of pride. But the truth is simpler and more uncomfortable: They were just human, like us, capable of both wonderful and terrible things.

If you've read any of my other books, you know I don't like talking about the demonic more than necessary. It's not because I'm afraid or think it's weird; it's because the best use of our attention is on God, His nature, and how to reflect Him. But I do think it's vital we understand how these principalities try to shape us—not so we can rebel against them but so we can notice them. So that when we feel their pull—when we feel ourselves idealizing someone, dismissing their faults, or demonizing them—we can pause and ask, "Where did this idea come from?" This isn't so we can get lost in introspection but so we can wrestle with it and take every thought captive. Let the Holy Spirit shape it. Align it more closely with God's kingdom.

These principalities aren't removed only through prayer. They lose ground when we change the structure they've been ruling from—first in our own hearts, then in our communities, and finally in our culture.

CHAPTER 8

MODERN EMPIRES

I'VE SPENT THE earlier chapters creating a shared set of language terms. We first discussed seeing in the spirit and how these visions are "visual poetry" designed to reveal spiritual truth, particularly God's nature. We're not only in a spiritual battle between angels and demons but also in spiritual structures of our own creation: empires great and small, built on the knowledge of good and evil.

None of these empires are fully good or fully bad. Many are formed from good intentions and parts of God's nature, but any structure, kingdom, or empire created by humans will inevitably produce injustice. Only the kingdom of God can produce true justice. We've also discussed how principalities seek to influence these empires and structures into forms that perpetuate destruction.

I'm reminding you of everything we've discussed so far because the next few stories are challenging. To understand these stories for what they are, you'll need to have a grasp on all the groundwork we've covered so far. We're created in God's image. We were created to be in His garden. We were exiled from that garden because we ate from the tree of the knowledge of good and evil. We began building cities and empires: imperfect and flawed imitations of God's kingdom on earth. We're still doing this today.

Every family, every church, every city, every business, every industry, every region, every country—every human structure—is an empire: a structure built on the knowledge of good and evil, not fully good or fully evil. Because we're made in the image of God, I believe we all naturally bend toward His nature, and many of the structures we create carry His goodness. Unfortunately, we're all also born into a world with sin in it. We weren't designed for this. We were designed for a garden. Being made for a garden but born into an empire has consequences.

THE NUANCE OF DECEPTION

Exploring the problem of empire—the problem of the knowledge of good and evil—requires a basic level of discernment to sense whether something is of a good or bad spirit. Higher discernment is required to perceive *why* a good or bad spirit is involved in a situation.

When God confronted Adam and Eve after they had eaten from the forbidden tree, both looked immediately for someone else to blame. Adam said, "The woman You gave to be with me, she gave me the fruit," blaming both

Eve and God for the outcome—nice one. Eve said, "The serpent deceived me," once more shifting the blame to an outside force. While it'd be untrue to say that Eve played no part in Adam eating the fruit, and the serpent played no part in Eve eating the fruit, no one in this story is willing to take responsibility for their own decision to eat from the forbidden tree.

As I share the next few stories, I encourage you to avoid the temptation to assign blame to anyone or any group. Instead, explore the nuance of deception. The story of the fall of mankind is about the influence of external spiritual forces, the influence people have on one another, and the choices we make as individuals. All these things contributed to the outcome in the garden, and they all contribute to the outcomes we experience today.

Without facing this complexity, we'll seek to blame rather than understand, as deciding on someone to blame is one of the fundamental impulses for anyone born into the knowledge of good and evil.

When I was in the fourth grade, my science teacher split the class into teams to build model bridges out of popsicle sticks, tape, and glue. My team spent a long time constructing an elaborate and beautiful suspension bridge. I was biased, of course, but I thought ours was the best-looking bridge in the class. The teacher proceeded to go to each popsicle stick bridge and place rocks on it until some part of the bridge buckled.

Some of the ramshackle bridges held only two or three rocks without breaking. One held over a dozen. When the teacher came to our bridge, I felt certain our masterpiece would hold more than any of them. You can imagine my dismay when, after the teacher placed a single rock in the center of it, the entire structure collapsed in on itself. As I stood there, trying to look like I wasn't heartbroken, my teacher said something that has stuck with me: "You can't know the integrity of a structure until weight has been put on it."

In March 2020, as the US began its first series of responses to the COVID-19 pandemic, I watched as weight was placed on a thousand different structures. Some bent, some buckled, and some broke down, as they hastily searched for anything to reinforce their straining structures.

CERTAINTY

I watched as the principality called Certainty pulled its many strings whenever I entered a conversation about the pandemic, just as I had in the airport when I watched people engage in social media. I saw dozens of strings emerge as a conspiracy-theorist friend went into over-drive, sharing theory after theory with me about why the pandemic was happening, who was behind it, and what their agenda might've been.

I watched dozens of strings emerge as a microbiologist friend explained each detail of the scientific response to COVID-19 and how anyone who didn't follow the recommended procedures was both ignorant and foolish. I watched as dozens of strings emerged from pastors, politicians, neighbors, friends, and family members, who shared their opinion about the pandemic. Even as I sat alone in my room, considering what my opinion about the pandemic might be—trying to integrate all the other opinions thrown in my direction—I watched as tiny little strings pulled at the skin on my arms.

You see, a principality like Certainty doesn't care about what you believe; it only cares that what you believe causes you to build an empire of your own design, because this'll always lead to destruction.

> YOU CAN'T KNOW THE INTEGRITY OF A STRUCTURE UNTIL WEIGHT HAS BEEN PUT ON IT.

Even now, as you read this book, you may be hoping the next few words will confirm your opinion about the pandemic, tempting you to twist these words to fit the narrative you've grown comfortable with—just a little tug here, a little twist there.

I'm not saying this impulse is caused by a demon. We like it when our opinions are validated. We like it when our empires are supported. The impulse comes from us, but the demonic seeks to take advantage of it, twisting it into something powerful enough to do great harm.

I watched these strings pull apart families, friendships, and churches. I watched these strings erupt from people's cell phones as they absorbed media designed to reinforce their beliefs. I watched Certainty twist people's lives apart. I'm sure you did too.

PRIDE

As the pandemic continued, I watched Pride at work too. One day, as I was walking into a store, I encountered a customer and a store clerk in an argument.

"I'm going to need you to put on a mask to enter the store, sir," the clerk said in a frustrated tone, indicating this wasn't the first time he had said it.

The customer's face flushed, and his eyes started to bulge. "I won't put that thing on my face, and you can't make me."

This was the first time I saw one of these arguments. They'd become so common that in the future I'd hardly take notice, but this time I stopped and watched the exchange at a distance—partially out of curiosity and partially because I was concerned it'd escalate to blows.

Between the two men, I saw Pride, as alluring and beautiful as ever. The principality held a tall golden sheet between the arguing men. I walked around with the pretense of grabbing a shopping cart, adjusting my perspective so I could see over the customer's shoulder at whatever was on that flat golden sheet.

It was like a semitransparent golden mirror. Through the gold sheet, I could see the store clerk, but I could also see a faint reflection of the customer. The worker was in his twenties, thirty or so pounds overweight, with soft features, pale skin, and dark hair with dyed blue tips. Through the golden sheet, however, he looked entirely different. The rippling sheet of thin gold altered his dimensions, making him look at least one hundred and twenty pounds overweight. His real expression was one of exhausted frustration, but through the golden sheet, he looked arrogant, petulant, and snide. Rather than blue-tipped hair, the sheet gave him a full head of rainbow-colored hair.

Though I try to carry honor and respect for all people, I felt a spike of judgment rising in me toward the store clerk. Despite my personal opinion—that masks were a minor inconvenience, which probably helped slow the spread of the pandemic—a defiance rose in me. This, however, was stifled immediately when I noticed how the golden sheet altered the customer's appearance.

In reality, the customer was middle-aged, wearing a light blue polo shirt, a ball cap with an American flag stitched into it, and had a strong but stocky build. He had probably been an athlete in high school or college but had softened with age. In the reflection of the sheet, he looked fifteen years younger, with a jaw more chiseled than it was in real life. In the reflection he looked calm, poised, and self-assured. In reality, his face was blotchy, and he was breathing awkwardly through his frustration.

I grabbed my shopping cart, slowly approached the pair of men, and took one of the face masks from the rack near the worker, who shot me a glance of exasperated thanks. The customer's eyes bulged in my direction, and he pressed his lips together more firmly. This new angle gave me a brief opportunity to see through the golden sheet from the other side. It looked just as I had expected.

From this perspective the customer looked like he was three seconds away from giving himself a stroke. His face was bright red and utterly defiant. He was several inches shorter and heavier, his clothes looked like what you'd see if you typed "redneck" into Google Image Search. His hat bore a Confederate flag.

From the worker's perspective, his own reflection looked more refined and intelligent. His hair was neat and his expression patient and cool—like the actor you'd cast to play the intelligent and long-suffering clerk standing for reason in the face of ignorance. Even though I was deeply aware of the game that Pride was playing, I still felt a surge of frustration rising in me. Wearing a mask wasn't much to ask. Why was this man being so belligerent? I shook it off as I pushed my cart past the two men, marveling at just how appealing pride can be.

The principality Pride didn't create the characteristic of pride in each of these men. Their pride was their own—the result of their internal empires—built on the knowledge of good and evil. I saw dozens of interactions like this over the next several months—some between strangers, some between friends, and some between families—all interactions and conflicts had Pride at the center.

In my state a statewide mandate to wear face masks never existed, so at our church we didn't require it. This meant that some people wore masks to church, and some didn't. As the pandemic wore on, I often saw Pride at the back of our church. Increasingly, I would see people enter our services wearing a pair of golden sunglasses made of the same material as that golden sheet. These glasses covered the eyes of people wearing face masks just as often as those who chose not to wear them. However, I often saw people wearing these glasses shoot disparaging glances at one another—looks of mutual judgment.

I hadn't been wearing a mask at church, but one week I decided to conduct an experiment and put on a face mask as I entered the sanctuary. In the first fifteen minutes, I counted nineteen disapproving looks and eight looks of approval. Nineteen glances seemed to say, "How could you? I thought you were one of us. What are you doing? Ugh, another sheep." Eight glances seemed to say, "You're with us. That's right. Good job. Well done. Blake is on our side. I'm so relieved." Each of these people, on both sides of the debate, were wearing the same golden sunglasses.

Years later, after much research on the effectiveness of face masks had been released, we had many more facts than we did at the start of the pandemic. Based on my conversations with others, how you interpret these facts and what they say about whether we should or shouldn't have worn face masks during the pandemic largely depends on what empire you're from.

DIVISION

As the pandemic wore on, so too did the pressure. More rocks were on a dozen different popsicle stick bridges. Cultural and political tensions continued to rise. I was part of the senior leadership at our church at the time. The church had always attracted a broad array of people, and this facet of our microculture—one I had always considered a strength—was proving to be a weakness under the weight of the pandemic and the resulting cultural strain.

Friendships were broken; people left our church to attend others or to start others; and every decision our team made was either too much, too little, or heading in the wrong direction. I've been in church all my life. None of this was new, but it was happening faster and more virulently than I had ever seen it before.

The sheer scale of the political and social tension—the way this tension caused so much pain in my church, in my friends, and in my family—weighed on me deeply. So many opinions, so much historical pain, so much recent pain, so much cultural momentum and inertia collided—both on a large and small scale. It was overwhelmingly sad.

I'VE BEEN IN CHURCH ALL MY LIFE. NONE OF THIS WAS NEW, BUT IT WAS HAPPENING FASTER AND MORE VIRULENTLY THAN I HAD EVER SEEN IT BEFORE.

One day, as I was praying in my office, with this tension sitting heavy in my heart, I yelled out to God, "What's going on?"

I ask God a lot of questions, and I rarely get a straight answer. This time was an exception.

I can see in the spirit anytime I have a mind to look, but I don't see everything, and I don't see it all clearly. Most of what I see is semitranslucent and often indistinct. It gets clearer when I focus on it, but it's rarely 100 percent clear and almost never interferes with my ability to see the physical world—very handy when driving a car. This time, as I asked God a question amid my sadness and frustration, I went into an open vision— a vision that fully overtook my sight. I could still feel the chair underneath me, and I could still smell the cup of coffee on my desk, but all I could see was in the spirit.

In the vision I was high in the air—so high I could see the United States beneath me. I could see clouds drifting beneath me and the few major mountain ranges and rivers that my rough sense of geography was able to identify. I could also see two massive principalities.

They were so large that each could've moved across the entire continent in four or five strides, the tops of their heads scraping the stratosphere. Their skin was a sickly combination of dark blue and gray. Their bodies were twisted, sinister imitations of the human form. They each had a tall, craggy crown on their head.

As I saw them, the sorrow and frustration that had led me to burst out with my question deepened. I felt the pain of all the family tensions I had experienced over the past few months. I felt the confusion and tension I had faced as I mediated conversations between church members, married couples, and other church leaders. I felt the chaotic strain of all the political conflict, rising cultural pain, conspiratorial thinking, religious discord, and the endless opposing "certainty" that had marked the COVID-19 era.

I felt dread looking at these principalities and a profound sense of powerlessness. This was unusual and disturbing. Ordinarily, I have such a strong sense of God's infinite superiority that I'm not troubled by the sight of any principality, no matter how deeply it has embedded itself into the fabric of culture.

My eyes were drawn to the crowns on their heads, and I realized words were written on them. Across the forehead of one principality was the word *Republican*.

Across the forehead of the other principality was the word *Democrat*. My dread doubled—partially at the conclusions my mind jumped to at the sight of this and partially at the furious responses I expected to receive should I ever decide to share this vision with anyone.

Before the dread could send my head spinning any further, I noticed that each principality had another word written on the back of their crown. The one with the word *Republican* on the front had the word *Democrat* written on the back; the one with the word *Democrat* on the front had the word *Republican* written on the back. This initially added confusion to my growing sense of dread, but then I heard the Lord speak. His voice carried a gentleness so powerful that it immediately calmed the storm of emotions churning in my chest.

"Son," He said, "it's just a spirit of division."

The vision ended, but the deep sense of peace that had permeated His voice remained.

MODERN EMPIRES

Demons and principalities don't make you act. The colloquial phrase "the devil made me do it" was always intended as a joke. It's a flimsy excuse for the darker side of human nature—the part of our nature founded on the knowledge of good and evil. These entities may blow on the coals of your intention, but it's always *your* intention. Principalities do have power, but they only have the power we give them.

I chose to use what I saw during the COVID-19 pandemic as an example of modern empires because it's an excellent model of how these empires work and the problems their imperfections cause. Most conflict during that time, from a spiritual perspective, wasn't a clash between the powers of heaven and the powers of hell. Heaven has already won. What we experienced during that time, and what we still experience to this day, is a conflict between human empires. Every human culture, every human institution, and every human mode of thought is laced with the knowledge of good and evil. These empires will always produce injustice for some and justice for others; they'll produce good here and bad there.

> DEMONS AND PRINCIPALITIES DON'T MAKE YOU DO THINGS. THEY MAY BLOW ON THE COALS OF YOUR INTENTION, BUT IT'S ALWAYS *YOUR* INTENTION.

Even cultures modeled after God's kingdom will produce injustice, because the best we can manage to create is *part* of His kingdom. Part of His kingdom is not His kingdom. You could build a perfect house with perfectly sturdy framing, a perfect electrical system, and perfect plumbing, but if no power grid or sewage and water system are connected to it, living there will be far from a perfect experience.

Some churches emphasize the study of the Bible but emphasize less on the living presence of God in our daily lives. Others focus on experiencing God's presence and activating the gifts of the Spirit but emphasize less on the deep study of the Bible. Still others focus on building thriving communities of healthy people but place only limited emphasis on the deep study of the Bible and developing a personal knowledge of God's presence.

Every church, in one way or another, is like a house with a great electrical system but no sewage system or a house with comfortable rooms and a great view but no access to running water. I'm not trying to besmirch or demean the church. I love any institution that intends to carry on the legacy of Jesus and equip others to do the same. However, because every person has sinned and fallen short of the glory of God, every one of us has built a church that is, to one degree or another, an empire—a manifestation of our idea of what is good and evil.

I love my church. It has blessed hundreds—maybe even thousands—of people. I've watched people grow and mature, fall in love with one another, become more like Jesus—but I've also seen pain, discord, and destruction. Some results are due to diversions from God's kingdom in individuals or in culture, while others are due to diversions from God's kingdom in our church system.

I know what some of these diversions are, but most are invisible to me. Though it's always been my intention to lead my family and any group I'm leading in a way representative of God and His kingdom, some of what I believe to be right or how I believe things should be done is founded in my experience, my tradition, and my own values rather than God's. They're part of my empire, and I can't see them all, because my empire is so normal to me that it's usually invisible.

We'll spend some time in the final section of this book exploring how we can see these empires that are so normal to us that they're functionally invisible. For now, my main hope is that you have the courage to acknowledge their existence.

I love my family and many other families. I love my church and many other churches. I love my country and many other countries. But within my love I must recognize that they're all empires built on the knowledge of good and evil. Once again, this doesn't mean they're bad; it just means they're not God's kingdom—not yet anyway. Many of them contain parts of God's kingdom—maybe even large parts—but they're still in need of much refining.

> WHERE YOU ARE IS EXACTLY WHERE YOUR EMPIRE LED YOU TO BE.

Principalities don't produce culture. They feed on it. They blow on the coals of our intention and our will to impose our knowledge of good and evil on the world. They perpetuate the destruction we've wreaked by our own hands.

Business writer Michael Gerber once wrote that "every system is perfectly designed to get the results it gets."[1] This principle is true of all human empires. This is how you can tell that your family, your church, and your country aren't perfect systems. Regardless of what you think or believe they're meant to produce, they're designed to produce what they've produced. Whatever results have come from your family, your church, your business, your school, your devotional group, your country, or your political party—this is the fruit of your empire. Where you are is exactly where your empire led you to be.

We can make the same mistake as Adam and Eve when

faced with the results of our empire, blaming a spiritual enemy or one another for these results. Though these external forces undoubtedly contribute to our outcomes, this blame disconnects us from our greatest power: the power of our own choices. Only by being willing to avoid the temptation to shift blame and by accepting responsibility for the results of our empire can we hope to get the feedback we need—and learn how to stop contributing to our own empires and to start building God's kingdom.

CHAPTER 9

ENGAGING PRINCIPALITIES

WHEN I WAS sixteen, I went to the movie theater with a group of friends. At the time a film was playing that a lot of people in the Christian community didn't like. They felt like it promoted some harmful ideas. In fact, a few churches had organized protests to fight against it.

When we arrived at the theater, I saw a group of the protesters standing outside. They carried homemade signs, chanted improvised rhymes, and blasted loud music. When I looked in the spirit, I saw a roaring fire around the group of protesters. It was as if each person was a piece of wood in a huge bonfire.

Above them, I saw a demonic principality. It was shaped like a bird, with dark feathers, hovering in the air with its wings spread wide enough to cover the entire entryway to the theater.

At first this seemed pretty straightforward—a group of Christians standing against something they thought was wrong. The fire must have been their spiritual fervor, trying to change the atmosphere, but the principality was resisting them.

As I looked closer, I realized much more was happening.

I noticed the fire had two distinct colors that twisted and moved around one another. One was a bright, glowing orange—pleasant to look at. The other was a deep, dark red—sickly and wrong, like the color of infection.

As they shook their signs and chanted, the fire would swirl and the colors would mix. In the flames I saw symbols and shapes appear. Some were good: a shining cross, an angel reaching out with compassion, and even the image of Jesus' face—kind and loving.

The images in the darker red of the fire looked entirely different. The cross loomed over the crowd entering the theater in a threatening, almost imperious way. The angel looked as if it were about to strike people with its fist. Jesus' face was contorted in a shout of rage.

I noticed that the heat of the fire was creating an updraft. The principality above the crowd used that heat to maintain its position, almost feeding on what was happening. I thought I saw a look of satisfaction on its face, as if it were nourished by the whole scene.

I tried to look more closely at the people in the crowd. In the spirit some were wearing beautiful, shining armor, and holding gleaming swords in the air. Others wore shabby, dirty robes and shook pitchforks or held torches.

As people walked toward the movie theater, I saw different reactions. Some were struck by a sense of conviction. Their posture changed as a lick of the orange flame touched them. That conviction seemed to have a positive effect. But others carried their own torches, and the flame from the protesters' fire made those torches burn even brighter. Their torches were made of the darker red part of the flame.

I stood there for a while, trying to sort out what I was seeing, as we waited for our tickets. Then, on the ground in front of the theater, I noticed what looked like a small art installation. It was an abstract spiritual sculpture, surrounded by carefully arranged flowers.

THE AUTHOR'S INTENT

The sculpture neither looked heavenly nor demonic. It did, however, look beautiful. Though I didn't know much about the movie that the group of Christians were protesting, I knew enough to recognize that this small sculpture was done in the same style as the movie's aesthetic.

I asked, "Lord, what is that?"

He said, "That is the author's intent."

I immediately thought of what I had learned in English class about author's intent: the message the creator wants to communicate through their work. While this particular piece wasn't fully godly, it also wasn't demonic. It was just *beautiful*.

I felt an odd discomfort about the protest, and what

I was seeing in the spirit made me feel even more uneasy. Because the movie my friends and I came to see aligned with a showing of this other film, I made note of several people so I could compare them on the way in and out.

I saw some theatergoers with demonic images around them, matching the movie's negative messages. Sure enough, some came out with those things looking stronger, better fed. But honestly, they were the minority. Most people came out looking pretty much the same as they did when they went in.

As we left, I noticed the protesters were still there. That same complex, tangled tapestry of good and bad was happening in the spirit around them. The fire blazed on, its updraft lifting the principality that hovered above them.

I looked again at that little sculpture on the ground—the image of the author's intent—and I felt sad. I didn't feel this way because I thought the movie was good or that it was getting unfair treatment. Instead, I was moved because this thing, even though it wasn't fully of God's kingdom, was beautiful. It seemed somehow wasteful to let the sculpture go ignored.

I looked up at the principality and asked, "Lord, what is that?"

He answered, "That is Profit."

This was the first time I saw this particular principality, but it was far from the last. It occurred to me that this was a major movie release—a big box office draw. That principality wasn't really tied to any demonic message in the movie itself. It was part of a much larger cultural system—one that seeks profit at any cost, regardless of moral value or purpose.

While I wouldn't want to judge the motives of the people at that protest or the group as a whole, I could see that, whatever their intentions, their actions were actually feeding that larger system. This ruling authority tried to perpetuate its own vision of "kingdom" on the earth.

WARRING EMPIRES

I spent a lot of time afterward reflecting on the relationship between the Christians' good intentions, the possible negative messages in the film, and how they all fed into a bigger problem.

What made me saddest about it was that little piece of the author's intent on the ground—that small, beautiful sculpture that everyone ignored. It was a piece of creativity lost in the conflict between warring empires.

HOW CAN GOD'S KINGDOM SPREAD IF WE'RE DISCONNECTED FROM THE WORLD?

As Christians we're likely to find ourselves in conflict with the culture around us. But how should we engage in such a conflict? Should we disengage from any ungodly culture? Perhaps, but isolating ourselves doesn't create many opportunities to influence culture. How can God's kingdom spread if we're disconnected from the world?

Should we try to obtain political power and direct culture? Maybe, but Jesus presented power in His kingdom in a way quite different from how we build and obtain power in earthly kingdoms. It seems that this approach would result in our perpetuating another kingdom of our own, rather than the kingdom of heaven.

In trying to make sense of the vision at the movie theater—and many other experiences of seeing in the spirit—I've wrestled with how easy it is to perpetuate the very structures we seek to overcome. In the final section of this book, I'll outline what I believe to be the biggest key to perpetuating God's kingdom without mistakenly creating a kingdom of our own. First, I'll outline three principles, postures that help set our minds and hearts to be ready to apply this key.

PRINCIPLE 1: RECOGNIZE NUANCE

As people we naturally like to simplify our understanding of the world: "This is good; this is bad; this is right; this is wrong."

While that kind of black-and-white thinking can be helpful—and while there really *are* good and bad things— it's also important to recognize that people are always a combination of good and bad, and they become this way for nuanced reasons.

When it came to that movie, my church community would likely have judged it as simply a *bad movie*. That conclusion might even have been correct, but saying it so absolutely leaves no room to recognize that there might've been good things in it. Good intent can result in bad outcomes, bad intent can lead to bad outcomes, and sometimes even bad intent can still produce something good. Most of the things people do have this kind of complexity.

If I had just shown up, seen Christians protesting the movie, noticed the fire around them, and seen a demon hovering in apparent opposition, I could've slotted it all neatly into tidy categories: *good Christians fighting a bad movie.* At that stage in my life, I didn't think much of Christians protesting things. Honestly, I looked down on it. Because of that perspective, when I saw the fire mixed with both good and bad imagery, I was quick to conclude it was my fellow Christians who were in the wrong.

I remember noticing the oppressive images in the fire—false pictures of Jesus, the threatening cross—and thinking those outweighed any of the good images. Seeing that the heat of the fire made it easier for the principality to stay aloft only reinforced my judgment that the whole thing was a net negative.

That, however, was me refusing to see the nuance. Even in that crowd, some people were genuinely motivated by care and concern, releasing pictures of God's kingdom into the environment. Even the ones whose imagery came out twisted or unhealthy might've not had any bad intentions. They were probably just doing what they had learned to do, without realizing the harmful effects.

We'll discuss this further in the next chapter, but at the end of the Book of Job, after arguing with his friends about whether good things happen to good people and bad things happen to bad people, God responds by pointing out the vastness of His creation. He essentially says, "You can't possibly hope to understand all of this."

To me, that's an invitation to recognize nuance—to admit the world is so complex that more than one thing can be true at once. Good intentions can lead to bad results, while bad intentions can sometimes lead to good results. If we don't accept that complexity, we'll misinterpret the things we see in the spirit or otherwise.

PRINCIPLE 2: ENGAGE WITH COMPASSION

The next principle that helps us interpret the spirit and the world well is learning to engage with compassion.

Initially, I engaged with judgment. I looked at the Christians protesting and judged their approaches, attitudes, and perspectives. I assumed the bad elements in their actions outweighed any good. Perhaps someone else would have been quicker to judge the filmmakers who produced the movie or the theatergoers who were watching it. But if we want to see as God sees, we must engage with compassion—not just to be "nice" but because of God's engagement with us.

God absolutely has boundaries and expectations for us. He asks us to align our behavior with His nature and a life committed to Him. At His core His engagement with us comes from compassion. Without this, relationship with Him wouldn't exist.

One of the most meaningful pictures of compassion to me is how a parent relates to their child. When I was a new father, if my three-year-old son misbehaved, I got scared. "Oh no, I have a bad kid! I must be doing something wrong."

Now that I have five kids, and I'm a more mature father, I see things differently. I see a child beginning to learn how to manage big feelings and how to treat others well. When my youngest daughter throws a tantrum or hits a sibling, I don't excuse or ignore the behavior, but I see it in the context of her development.

Compassion doesn't mean ignoring the wrong; it means seeing the whole picture, recognizing and accepting human limits. It means meeting someone where they are while challenging them to be who they were meant to be. Compassion is a product of maturity.

Over the years, as I let the Holy Spirit reshape my understanding of that vision, I found myself growing in compassion for those at the protest. They were scared what that movie might do, worried about its influence on children. Maybe I would have responded differently. But they responded the best way they knew how. Many acted out of genuine love for God's kingdom.

PRINCIPLE 3: OBSERVE THE CONSEQUENCES OF YOUR BELIEFS

Another principle I have grown to treasure more and more is the importance of observing the consequences produced by our beliefs.

As we form our understanding of the world and spiritual things, we must discipline ourselves to pay attention to how our thinking plays out in reality.

My initial thought was that these Christians were being foolish and that their protest was pointless. But where did that belief lead? It made me bitter toward my fellow Christians. It made me judgmental. One reason I kept asking the Holy Spirit for help understanding this vision was that I recognized those outcomes didn't match His nature. So I asked Him to correct me.

I don't know whether the people who planned or attended that protest dialogued with the Holy Spirit about their experience. I hope they did. Many Christians go through their lives with an "us versus the world" mindset. While the values of God's kingdom and the values of the world are often in opposition, we must be willing to observe the consequences of an overemphasis on this conflict. Maybe certain groups and individuals could be considered our enemies, but we're called to love our enemies. We follow a Savior who loved the world so much He gave His life for it (John 3:16).

IF WE WANT TO TRANSFORM THE WORLD, THE BEST WAY TO START IS BY BEING TRANSFORMED OURSELVES.

If our way of thinking produces bitterness, division, fear, or a diminished view of God's power, it's worth reexamining. We can't afford to ignore these consequences; otherwise, we'll be unable to see whether what we're doing and thinking leads to the fruit of God's kingdom.

Recognizing nuance helps us acknowledge the need for humility: to admit we can't comprehend the world's complexity as God does. This makes us dependent on His perspective. Engaging with compassion challenges us to be motivated by the same love that led Jesus to the cross. This makes us dependent on His nature. Observing the consequences of our beliefs ensures we're not blind to the areas where we're missing the mark. This makes us dependent on His truth.

Each of these principles requires us to be transformed by God's nature. If we want to transform the world, the best way to start is by being transformed ourselves.

CHAPTER 10

THE WAY OF WISDOM

WHEN I WAS a teenager, I went with my parents to a conference in Florida. It was a typical charismatic, Christian gathering: Different people taught on various subjects—some on the prophetic, others on the kingdom of God. While I enjoyed most of the teaching, one teacher rubbed me the wrong way.

At that stage of life, my late teens, I was a little jaded. I had grown up in the church and had realized that Christians' good intentions didn't always match the outcomes in their lives or in the lives of those they led.

This particular preacher was teaching on prosperity. He taught about how God wants you to have good things and wants you to be wealthy. He even claimed that Christians should be the wealthiest people on the planet.

Maybe it was because of my missionary background, but this message had never sat well with me. It's not that I disagreed with the idea that God wants good things for us. Of course, money can bring stability and support our happiness, and it can be used to benefit others. But the way these messages were typically emphasized—with so much gusto and so little nuance—made me feel like something was off.

Midway through the sermon, this preacher shared the story of Jesus and the rich man from Mark 10. The following is the part that he read:

> As Jesus was starting out on his way to Jerusalem, a man came running up to him, knelt down, and asked, "Good Teacher, what must I do to inherit eternal life?"
>
> "Why do you call me good?" Jesus asked. "Only God is truly good. But to answer your question, you know the commandments: 'You must not murder. You must not commit adultery. You must not steal. You must not testify falsely. You must not cheat anyone. Honor your father and mother.'"
>
> "Teacher," the man replied, "I've obeyed all these commandments since I was young."
>
> Looking at the man, Jesus felt genuine love for him. "There is still one thing you haven't done," he told him. "Go and sell all your possessions and give the money to the poor, and you will have treasure in heaven. Then come, follow me."
>
> At this the man's face fell, and he went away sad, for he had many possessions.
>
> Jesus looked around and said to his disciples, "How hard it is for the rich to enter the Kingdom of God!" This amazed them. But Jesus said again, "Dear children, it is very hard to enter the Kingdom

of God. In fact, it is easier for a camel to go through the eye of a needle than for a rich person to enter the Kingdom of God!"

—MARK 10:17–25, NLT

TWISTING THE SCRIPTURES

At this point, the preacher paused and said, "Let me give you some historical context."

He explained that a gate into Jerusalem called the "Eye of the Needle" existed, which was narrow and low. Merchants with camels heavily loaded with goods would have to either unload the baggage or have the camel kneel to enter. He suggested that Jesus didn't mean wealth was incompatible with the kingdom—only that wealth should be approached with an attitude of submission.

I wasn't buying it.

Maybe it was my teenage angst. Maybe it was my spiritual discernment. As he kept talking, I noticed something in the spirit. Behind the preacher I saw an all-too-familiar principality peeking into the room—the large, dark, birdlike creature I had come to know as Profit.

As the sermon went on, I saw an image forming behind the preacher. It was a picture of Jesus but not like any I had ever seen. This Jesus was tall and handsome, dressed in royal purples, rich golds, and deep blues. He wore many rings and an ornate crown. However, something in his eyes was off. His expression was haughty; his demeanor was almost prideful.

It was a Jesus dressed in wealth and power, but his attitude didn't feel like Jesus at all. He looked around the room with disdain, a down-the-nose posture that didn't match anything I had ever experienced in the real Jesus. Though the preacher never outright said that wealth equaled righteousness, his message edged dangerously close to that idea—that having more was a sign of Christian character and having less was a sign of a character deficit.

Profit kept poking in from the side, inspecting the scene with something that looked almost like satisfaction.

When I got home, I did some research. As it turns out, no archaeological evidence exists for any gate in Jerusalem called the Eye of the Needle. In fact, many scholars point out how impractical such a gate would have been and note that, even if there were a small gate, plenty of others would have been easier to use.

THIS WASN'T HISTORICAL CONTEXT, BUT RATHER IT WAS A MANUFACTURED ANECDOTE USED TO SOFTEN THE CLEAR MESSAGE OF JESUS.

More importantly, the grammar in the passage uses the indefinite article—"an eye of a needle"—indicating a metaphorical sewing needle, not a specific location. This is also true in the original language.

This wasn't historical context, I concluded, but rather it was a manufactured anecdote used to soften the clear message of Jesus. If we keep reading the passage where the preacher left off, the picture becomes even clearer:

> The disciples were astounded. "Then who in the world can be saved?" they asked.
> Jesus looked at them intently and said, "Humanly

speaking, it is impossible. But not with God. Everything is possible with God."

Then Peter began to speak up. "We've given up everything to follow you," he said.

"Yes," Jesus replied, "and I assure you that everyone who has given up house or brothers or sisters or mother or father or children or property, for my sake and for the Good News, will receive now in return a hundred times as many houses, brothers, sisters, mothers, children, and property—along with persecution. And in the world to come that person will have eternal life. But many who are the greatest now will be least important then, and those who seem least important now will be the greatest then."

—MARK 10:26–31, NLT

Jesus' answer didn't offer a caveat to justify the man's value for his wealth. Instead, He pointed out the simple truth of all heavenly transformation: Only God makes it possible. Only God changes the heart. Just as importantly, the value systems of the kingdom don't always match the value systems of the world. In fact, they often run counter to one another.

The message Jesus taught wasn't about wealth itself being wrong but about how our hearts relate to it. The preacher I heard that day, in my opinion, was trying to reshape Jesus' words to suit his own goals—a message not rooted in the kingdom but in his own values, values that seemed to please a principality.

I'm not saying every person who preaches prosperity is led by a principality. But these kinds of messages often get entangled in cultural values, in personal expectations, and in unseen influences. This is why it's so important to stay thoughtful and to test what we hear against the actual nature of Jesus.

This preacher wasn't delivering the worst version of the prosperity gospel I've ever heard. But the subtlety of the message was exactly what made it feel dangerous. Sometimes the enemy doesn't need a loud lie—just a small twist.

This is how our empires grow more corrupt and how we divert from our assignment to perpetuate God's kingdom on earth. The moment we chose in the garden to decide what was right and wrong for ourselves, we set a course for generations of systems, cultures, and values built on that independence. These empires shape the way we think, feel, and live.

While our own self-righteousness, self-defense, self-pity, or selfishness is more than enough to divert these empires from the model of the kingdom Jesus represented, they're also warped by the influence of demons and principalities. Both our own self-interest and demonic influence warp our internal empires, including how we perceive the model of God's kingdom in Jesus.

FALSE IMAGES OF JESUS

This isn't the only time I've seen false pictures of Jesus. In fact, I've seen them quite often. When I have visited churches or have conversations with other Christians, these images show up. While they're not wildly wrong or cartoonishly evil, they're retouched, remodeled, and altered just enough to highlight the traits we want Jesus to affirm, rather than the traits He actually embodies. These images reflect our values more than His.

I've seen these false pictures of Jesus show up in the way we think about political issues, immigration, LGBTQ culture, education, the treatment of the poor, and even how we should support the people of Israel. I've seen them when we talk about family, when we teach about marriage, parenting, submission, and leadership. I've seen their influence on the design of our churches and the values we elevate. While I could continue to unpack specific examples, I think it's much more helpful to focus on training ourselves

ARE WE TRYING TO BEND JESUS INTO AFFIRMING OUR VALUES OR ALLOWING HIS NATURE TO RESHAPE OUR MINDS AND HEARTS?

always to ask this question: "Are we trying to bend Jesus into affirming our values or allowing His nature to reshape our minds and hearts?" Even if the values are correct, if we're bending the nature of Jesus to affirm them, we're putting a flaw in our structure that'll lead to its collapse later in our lives or in future generations.

I also know I don't have a perfect image of who Jesus is or what it means to follow Him rightly. However, when someone reacts with outrage or emotional shutdown at the mere *suggestion* that their picture of Jesus might not be accurate, it's usually a sign they're more attached to their version of Jesus than to Jesus Himself.

Most of us have seen thousands of images—literal and figurative—of what it looks like to follow Jesus. They pop up on social media every day. But when you hear something that brings you comfort or that reaffirms what you already believe, take a moment. Ask yourself, "Is this comfort coming from alignment with the heart of Jesus? Or is it just the comfort that comes from seeing a reflection of myself?"

Ask yourself, "Do my decisions—how I live, how I vote, how I parent, and how I worship—truly reflect the message of God's kingdom? Or are these all reflections of the empire I've grown up in, the one I've helped build, and the one I created in rebellion to the one I came from?"

Later in this book, we'll discuss how to posture our hearts to follow Jesus. But for now, I encourage you to continually ask yourself this question: "Am I submitted to the teachings and person of Jesus, or have I created an idol in His image—something familiar, something comforting—which isn't Him?" This isn't something you can ask once and be done. It's a question you'll be asking for the rest of your life. I know I will.

Even the disciples who walked with Him constantly misunderstood Jesus—even right up until His death and resurrection. Peter, one of His closest friends, still made mistake after mistake, misjudging the application of Jesus' teachings. That's OK. It's not about being mistake-free. It's about having a heart oriented toward Jesus, saying yes to being corrected, yes to being shaped, and yes to seeing more clearly.

WALKING IN WISDOM

If we really want to understand how we're meant to live as spiritual people in a physical world—ambassadors of His kingdom—then we need a foundation. That foundation must be the person of Jesus. He is the purest example of what it means to bring God's kingdom to earth. He is the One who constantly taught about what the kingdom of heaven is like. He is the living fulfillment of that original commission in the garden: to cultivate, to steward, and to spread life. This isn't an empire but a kingdom.

One tool that helps us walk this out is wisdom. In the Bible we're given several books often referred to as "wisdom literature." Wisdom, in the Hebrew sense, isn't just cleverness or knowledge; it's experiential, grounded, spiritual intelligence. It's insight that harmonizes with the way God made the world to work. One definition I love—given to me by one of my teachers when I was first learning how to study the Bible—is this: Wisdom is the intelligence by which the Lord made the world to work together.

While the entire Scripture is full of wisdom, and many key books make up the wisdom literature, including Psalms and Song of Solomon, we'll explore three particular books to try to capture a framework for wisdom: Proverbs, Ecclesiastes, and Job.

Again, I'm not a theologian or biblical scholar. I'm just a lifelong student of the Bible. So this brief exploration of these three books is less an exhaustive breakdown than an invitation to hunger for more—a short representation of how the truths found within them have changed my way of thinking. As we explore these books, we discover different angles of wisdom. Some are intuitive. Others push against our natural thinking. But taken together, they form a fuller picture of how to live well in the kingdom.

Proverbs

The Book of Proverbs is probably the most well-known of the wisdom books. Much of it is direct, practical, and encouraging. It paints a beautiful picture of how the world *should* work. It says, "If you do this, good things will happen." Proverbs is full of bite-sized truths that help us build a life of wisdom, righteousness, and blessing.

Wisdom in Proverbs is often personified as "Lady Wisdom," a radiant, mysterious figure calling us to listen, heed her voice, and seek her out. If Proverbs was written today, it would, in some ways, be equivalent to those best-selling books you see while scrolling on Instagram or watching a talk show. Its author would probably have their own TED Talk, and several clips from it would go viral every other week. Proverbs is clear, hopeful, and beautifully structured.

Some of its gems include the following:

- "Who can find a virtuous and capable wife? She is more precious than rubies" (Prov. 31:10, NLT).

- "Guard your heart above all else, for
  it determines the course of your life"
  (Prov. 4:23, NLT).

- "The heartfelt counsel of a friend is as sweet
  as perfume and incense" (Prov. 27:9, NLT).

- "Love prospers when a fault is forgiven,
  but dwelling on it separates close friends"
  (Prov. 17:9, NLT).

- "The tongue can bring death or life; those
  who love to talk will reap the consequences"
  (Prov. 18:21, NLT).

Of course, woven all throughout the book is this central theme: The fear of the Lord is the beginning of wisdom.

The fear of the Lord has little to do with being scared of God in the way we might fear a predator, an aggressive person, or impending doom. This kind of fear is more akin to how we feel when we stand at the precipice of a massive waterfall, when we realize how much we have to learn when studying a new subject, or when we discover just how big our galaxy is and how many millions of galaxies exist far beyond our reach. The fear of the Lord happens when we begin to see how big God truly is—how "bigness" can only be a primitive metaphor for the immensity of His nature.

The fear of the Lord is what happens when we abide in the knowledge that He is God and we are not.

The phrase "fear of the Lord" occurs fourteen times

in the Book of Proverbs. The concept appears twenty to twenty-five times, depending on who you ask. It's addressed in the first chapter of Proverbs as the book describes its own purpose:

> The proverbs of Solomon son of David, king of Israel: for gaining wisdom and instruction; for understanding words of insight; for receiving instruction in prudent behavior, doing what is right and just and fair; for giving prudence to those who are simple, knowledge and discretion to the young— let the wise listen and add to their learning, and let the discerning get guidance—for understanding proverbs and parables, the sayings and riddles of the wise.
>
> The fear of the LORD is the beginning of knowledge, but fools despise wisdom and instruction.
>
> —PROVERBS 1:1–7

I won't linger too long on Proverbs because many of us have already spent time in this book. Hopeful, inspiring, and deeply rooted in truth, it's popular for a reason. But here's the thing: If we don't read Proverbs alongside the *other* books of wisdom, we risk distorting its message. If we ignore the other wisdom books—and a few of Proverbs's own allusions to the nuance and depth of wisdom—we could mistakenly create a formulaic view of God's wisdom, a simple "do this and get that" mentality. We can start to think that following God always results in immediate blessing, turning what is meant to be a relationship as complex and dynamic as any other into a transactional exchange—a blessing vending machine.

Ecclesiastes

If Proverbs embodies the bright-eyed young optimist—full of sharp observations about how life works—then Ecclesiastes is more like a deeply intelligent, middle-aged teacher who has seen a lot, been let down a few too many times, and learned to smile wryly at the optimist's enthusiastic ideas. Ecclesiastes is a bit of an outlier in the collection of biblical wisdom literature: a little sarcastic, often somber, and at times even borderline depressing. Despite this it's one of my favorite books in the Bible.

The book is framed with an interesting structure. A curator or commenter bookends the book—first with a brief introduction to the book's main author, the Preacher, and at the end with some brief commentary. What about the Preacher? Well, He starts with a bang:

> "Futility of futilities," says the Preacher, "Futility of futilities! All is futility."
>
> What advantage does a person have in all his work which he does under the sun? A generation goes and a generation comes, but the earth remains forever. Also, the sun rises and the sun sets; and hurrying to its place it rises there again. Blowing toward the south, then turning toward the north, the wind continues swirling along; and on its circular courses the wind returns. All the rivers flow into the sea, yet the sea is not full. To the place where the rivers flow, there they flow again. All things are wearisome; no

one can tell it. The eye is not satisfied with seeing, nor is the ear filled with hearing. What has been, it is what will be, and what has been done, it is what will be done. So there is nothing new under the sun. Is there anything of which one might say, "See this, it is new"? It has already existed for ages which were before us. There is no remembrance of the earlier things, and of the later things as well, which will occur, there will be no remembrance of them among those who will come later still.

—ECCLESIASTES 1:2–11, NASB

This word translated as "futility"—some translations say, "meaningless," while others say, "vanity"—appears thirty-eight times in this relatively short book. The Hebrew word is *hevel*, which means "mist" or "vapor." It becomes a kind of poetic refrain: a whisper, a sigh, a breath on a cold morning—there, then gone. That's the picture the Teacher uses to express the enigmatic, the transitory, the inconsistent, and the ironic.

It's not that life is meaningless in the nihilistic sense. It's that life is elusive, mysterious, and hard to grab onto. Sometimes events happen that don't make sense, and the more you try to nail it all down, the more it slips through your fingers. Ecclesiastes walks right up to the carefully laid truths of Proverbs, looks them over with a raised eyebrow, and asks, "OK, but what about when it doesn't work?"

The Teacher tells stories—stories about a good man who works hard and leaves everything to his kids only for them to waste it, and stories about a wicked man who prospers and never seems to suffer for it. It's a book full of the quiet frustration we all feel at times. I did what I was supposed to do, so why didn't it work?

It's not exactly the message you embroider on a pillow or turn into a motivational poster, which is probably why Ecclesiastes doesn't get nearly as much love as Proverbs. But if you've ever done everything right and still had the floor fall out from under you, you know why this book matters.

What I've always loved about Ecclesiastes is that it doesn't flinch. It doesn't pretend. It doesn't offer shallow answers. It just sits with you in the ache and says, "Yeah, I see it too." That's oddly comforting, especially when it's God doing the sitting.

Yet, for all its tension, Ecclesiastes doesn't end in despair. It ends in reverence. The curator or commenter steps back in at the end and says, "Yes, the Teacher's words can be sharp—like a goad, like a stick a shepherd uses to keep the sheep moving—but they're worth listening to." Then, he says something beautifully simple: "Here's the conclusion: Fear God. Keep His commandments."

In other words, life is misty, strange, and sometimes unfair. You won't always understand why things

ECCLESIASTES WALKS RIGHT UP TO THE CAREFULLY LAID TRUTHS OF PROVERBS, LOOKS THEM OVER WITH A RAISED EYEBROW, AND ASKS, "OK, BUT WHAT ABOUT WHEN IT DOESN'T WORK?"

happen the way they do. But even in that uncertainty, walk in wisdom. Follow God—not because it always makes life easy, but because it aligns you with something greater, truer, and more eternal than your momentary circumstances.

I remember the first time that idea really landed for me. It felt like God was sitting next to me—not to explain away the mess but to acknowledge it and to say, "Yeah, I see it too. I'm not ignoring it. But I'm still good. And it's still worth following Me."

That's what Ecclesiastes does. It gives us permission to wrestle, to wonder, and to still choose to follow. It challenges us to hold both mystery and reverence at the same time. In that tension we discover a deeper kind of wisdom: one that doesn't demand tidy answers but rests in a God who knows, even when we don't. It acknowledges and affirms the acute pain of sitting in the truth that He is God and we are not.

Job

Last—and maybe most mysterious—we have the Book of Job.

I've heard pastors wrestle with Job from just about every angle, and I can see why: It reads unlike any other story in the Bible. The language is poetic and sweeping, the events hard to grapple with, and the implications of the story difficult to nail down.

In fact, some theologians have suggested that Job might not be a literal record of actual events but a kind of divine thought experiment or a morality tale. The story opens with the line, "There was a man in the land of Uz," which some scholars suggest is similar to the phrase "Once upon a time." But to me, whether this story is literal doesn't take away from its power. Its message still hits just as hard, and its questions still matter just as much. Parts of the Bible are literal, parts are historical, and parts are poetic or literary—but they all reveal truth.

The book opens with an unusual scene: God encounters a figure who challenges Him regarding His servant Job. Most translations of the Bible identify this figure as Satan, but the Hebraic grammar used suggests that this isn't the devil. In Hebrew the title is *Ha-Satan*, "the satan, the accuser," a job description. Many biblical scholars have implied that this figure isn't the great adversary—the devil—but a kind of auditor or prosecuting lawyer, someone who works for God. I'll let you study to derive your own conclusions, but I present this to press against the idea that many get when reading the introduction to this book—that Job is somehow a pawn in a contest between God and the devil.

What unfolds in the opening chapters is one of the most intense calamities in Scripture. Job loses everything: his children, his wealth, and his health. He's reduced to sitting in the dust, covered in sores, and scraping at his skin with broken pottery. His wife gives up on him, and then his friends show up.

Now I'm using "friends" loosely, because what they bring isn't comfort. What they bring is a theological debate. While they say many things over a dozen chapters, their speeches all boil down to the same basic argument: God is just. In their view justice means that good things happen to people who do good things, and bad things happen to people who do bad things. Therefore, they believe that Job must have done something to deserve this misfortune.

Job pushes back. "I've searched my heart," he says again and again. "I've lived righteously. I've honored God. I don't understand why this is happening." But his so-called friends won't let up. Their logic doesn't leave room for mystery. They've eaten from the tree of knowledge, and they've decided they know exactly how good and evil work.

The conversations are long, becoming redundant and repetitive. Yet this, I believe, is intentional. The Book of Job reveals what occurs when we attempt to explain suffering through human reasoning. Round and round we go, trying to fit everything into a system we control—a system where the righteous are always rewarded and the wicked always fall.

Then—finally—God shows up.

He doesn't answer his friends. He neither confirms nor denies their claims about how justice works. Instead, God speaks from the whirlwind, unleashing a series of questions so poetic and powerful that each time I read them, I'm tempted to learn Hebrew just to hear how they originally sounded.

God doesn't give Job an explanation. What He gives is something better: Himself. For a moment God pulls back the curtain just a little and shows Job a glimpse of creation's vastness, the universe's mysteries, and the sheer magnitude of all He has made. In doing so, God reminds Job—and us—how much we will never fully grasp.

In summary God's answer is this: "I am God; you are not."

What I appreciate most about Job's response is its freedom from fear or shame. It's not groveling. The words Job uses to say, "I stand corrected," are tender. They come from the kind of intimacy you would find between a son and a loving parent or a student and a trusted mentor. It's a response of reverence, yes, but also of comfort.

Then, in the end, Job's fortunes are restored. He receives more children, more wealth, and more years of prosperous life. But the story doesn't undo the loss. His first children are still gone. That part of the story doesn't get erased. That's important because life isn't always a neat restoration. Some things aren't replaceable—even God doesn't pretend otherwise.

The book closes with this line: "And Job died, an old man and full of days" (Job 42:17, NASB).

To me, that phrase "full of days" carries so much weight. It speaks of a life lived in its fullness, with all its joys and griefs. It's the life of a man who walked with God—not just through blessings but through devastation. It's the life of a man who came out on the other side—still faithful, still listening, and still willing to wrestle with mystery.

If Proverbs is the voice of optimistic wisdom—bright, hopeful, and full of insight—and Ecclesiastes is the voice of middle-aged skepticism—sharp, weary, but still clinging to truth—then Job is the voice of the elder—tested and questioning but ultimately enduring. He's the one who lived through the storm and can still say, "He is good. Even when I don't understand, He is good."

Together, these three books form a whole picture of wisdom. They remind us that, yes, wisdom can lead to good things but not always in the way we expect. That, yes, we can live righteously, but suffering still comes. These books encourage us to pursue wisdom, but they all carry an essential balancing truth: You can't understand everything because He is God and we are not.

The fear of the Lord is the foundation of subverting our empires. It's an active rejection of the knowledge of good and evil. It's not willful ignorance: "I can't know what's good and evil, so I just need someone to tell me what to do." The fear of the Lord is alignment with the truth that He is God and we are not. It's the posture from which we must pursue all wisdom and knowledge if we want to be ambassadors of His kingdom rather than our own.

The fear of the Lord will make you immune to the influence of principalities. It'll produce a humility in you that'll grow into the three principles I addressed in the previous chapter: (1) learning to recognize nuance, (2) engaging with compassion, and (3) observing the consequences of your beliefs.

Developing the fear of the Lord is a lifelong practice, counterintuitive to the part of us that changed by eating from the wrong tree. But the fruit of it is well worth the effort.

A DIVINE PROGRESS REPORT

A few years ago, I was sitting in a camping chair in my garage while my kids played nearby, splashing each other with hoses and chasing each other around. I found myself wondering how I was doing as a parent. Parenting matters deeply to me. I put a lot of effort into it. I read books, ask questions, and learn from wiser people whenever I can. So I asked, "Lord, how am I doing? Give me a letter grade, a score—something." I don't usually think in those terms, but for whatever reason I did that day. The Lord responded right away.

"You're failing in ways that you couldn't possibly understand, even if I told you."

Though this may sound incredibly mean when reading it in plain text, this statement washed over me with deep comfort.

That moment gave me a visceral understanding of what Job must have felt at the end of his conversation with the Lord: corrected and comforted—not shamed, scolded, or dismissed but known, loved, and seen.

Of course I was failing. All parents do. I can't know how to be a perfect parent. Of course, God knows how to be a better Father than I ever could. Though I've committed a significant amount of time to growing as a parent, I've not grown enough to contain all that God knows about being a Father.

> THE FEAR OF THE LORD IS COUNTERINTUITIVE TO THE PART OF US THAT CHANGED BY EATING FROM THE WRONG TREE. BUT THE FRUIT OF IT IS WELL WORTH THE EFFORT.

That kind of insight only comes after you've walked with the Lord long enough—through joy, confusion, failure, and grace—to actually trust His voice, even when it says something that hurts. I wasn't hearing the voice of a harsh taskmaster. I wasn't pushed into shame. I was hearing the voice of a Father: the kind who disciplines because He delights in His children and who corrects because He wants us to become whole.

Many of us start out seeing God as harsh, disappointed, and critical of us. That view becomes reinforced by pastors, teachers, and even parents. But as we grow and mature, we come to see His tenderness, His kindness, His patience, and His joy in us.

But here's the catch: Sometimes when we finally let ourselves believe He's that good, we start to reject correction. We rest in our identity as sons and daughters of the King—which is right and good—but in that resting, we sometimes drift into passivity. We forget that our loving Father is also a holy God and that His love doesn't erase His righteousness, but rather it's an essential part of the same whole.

When we see this, we may be tempted to swing back into performance again, trying to earn His approval, live up to His standard, or wallow in shame when we miss the mark.

But there's another way, and it's not a swing between two extremes—it's a step forward.

It's a path where we integrate the truth that God remains loving and tender while being just and holy. God still has expectations and continues to correct us. Yet every ounce of correction is delivered from a heart of perfect love—a heart that never changes its affection for us and disciplines us only to deepen the connection.

This kind of rich connection is the only way to receive the transformation we need to grow into the kind of people who can transform the world.

PART IV
TRANSFORMING THE WORLD

IN THIS BOOK we've explored the concept of empire: grand spiritual structures that influence the whole world and everyone in it. We've discussed how principalities influence these structures toward even more destruction than they might've produced on their own. In this final section, we will explore how we can make a difference. If we're exiles from a garden living in a world full of empires and living to perpetuate God's kingdom on earth, how can we ensure we're spreading His kingdom rather than our own?

This book started with another question. One that arose when I watched five golden arrows fail to pierce my wayward friend. Why do some good things fail to pierce through the veil? Though these two questions may seem unrelated at first, the truth is that they're deeply intertwined, and their answers are rooted in the same profound truth.

Scan the QR code or visit BlakeHealyBooks.com/throughtheveil/resources to watch a short video introducing the themes you'll explore in this section.

CHAPTER 11

TWO PROPHETS

To UNDERSTAND HOW we can be effective ambassadors of God's kingdom, it's wise to first look at other ambassadors God's sent in the past. We'll be looking at two prophets, each sent to bring a message from God to an earthly empire. One was successful, and one was not. This is not only valuable because of the example these two prophets provide; it is also where I found my answer to the question of why those golden arrows failed to pierce my friend.

JONAH

Our first prophet is Jonah. This is a story familiar to many who grew up in church, but I think it's one that may be not incorrectly but often incompletely taught.

For those who don't know, the following is an abbreviated account of the story:

Jonah received a word from the Lord that he was to go to the city of Nineveh and deliver a prophetic word about coming judgment. At the beginning of the story, we don't know why, but Jonah refuses and goes in the opposite direction. He boards a boat heading away from where he's been told to go.

A great storm comes on the ship—one so terrible that the sailors fear for their lives. They're so terrified that they think some god must be causing it. They essentially ask, "Has anyone upset a god recently?" Jonah essentially says, "My God is the God of the wind and waves, and He did specifically tell me to do something that I did not do. You should probably just throw me into the ocean."

The sailors don't want to do that right away. (Good on them.) They try to row back to shore, but it doesn't work. Finally, with some trepidation, they essentially say, "Sorry, Jonah," and they toss him overboard. Rather than drowning, Jonah is swallowed by a great fish. This all happens in chapter 1.

In chapter 2 Jonah offers a prophetic prayer while waiting in the belly of the fish. He pulls elements from a few different psalms, praising God as a great Savior and rescuer, but he never quite apologizes for his disobedience. After this prayer, the fish spits him out on dry land.

In chapter 3 Jonah finally goes to Nineveh. It's said to be a great city, taking three days to walk across. Jonah walks one day into this journey and delivers what might be the worst prophetic sermon recorded in Scripture:

"Forty more days and Nineveh will be overthrown" (v. 4). That's it.

Despite this poor presentation, the response is immediate and powerful. People repent. This message reaches the king, who orders everyone to wear sackcloth and ashes and to fast. He even commands the animals to fast. Seeing this response, God decides not to let the promised calamity happen.

Now I want to zoom in on the end of this story in chapter 4, because it holds some important keys.

Most times when this story is taught, especially to children, it's presented as a lesson about obedience. God told Jonah to do something, he ran away, he suffered calamity, and then he obeyed. The end.

But if this were just a story about obedience, it should end at chapter 3. Jonah disobeyed and then obeyed. The word was delivered. Repentance happened. But that's not where it ends.

Chapter 4 begins with the following:

> But to Jonah this seemed very wrong, and he became angry. He prayed to the LORD, "Isn't this what I said, LORD, when I was still at home? That is what I tried to forestall by fleeing to Tarshish. I knew that you are a gracious and compassionate God, slow to anger and abounding in love, a God who relents from sending calamity. Now, LORD, take away my life, for it is better for me to die than to live."
>
> But the LORD replied, "Is it right for you to be angry?"
>
> —JONAH 4:1–4

This is alluding to a conversation that we didn't hear in the first chapter—a conversation that explains Jonah's motive. He ran away from Nineveh, not because he was scared, but because he knew God would be merciful.

It seems strange on the surface, but with some historical context, it makes more sense. Nineveh was the capital of the Assyrian Empire—an empire known for its brutal conquest. It ruled with an iron fist and proudly documented its cruel treatment toward those it conquered.

While we don't know whether Jonah personally suffered at its hands, he undoubtedly knew people who had. He knew its reputation. So when God asks, "Is it right for you to be angry?" we may not agree with Jonah's anger, but we can understand it.

Jonah doesn't answer God's question. Instead, he goes outside the city to sulk. He builds a shelter and waits to see what will happen. God provides a leafy plant to give him shade, and Jonah is happy about the plant. But the next day God sends a worm to chew it up. When the sun rises, God provides a scorching east wind, and Jonah grows faint and angry again.

God said to Jonah, "Is it right for you to be angry about the plant?"

"It is," he said. "And I'm so angry I wish I were dead" (v. 9).

The Lord said,

> You have been concerned about this plant, though you did not tend it or make it grow. It sprang up overnight and died overnight. And should I not have concern for the great city of Nineveh, in which

there are more than a hundred and twenty thousand people who cannot tell their right hand from their left—and also many animals?

—JONAH 4:10–11

The End.

The Book of Jonah has a surprisingly abrupt ending—like one of those artsy films with an obscure ending that leaves the plot unresolved. In literature an author may use an obscure ending when the story's meaning isn't found in the plot's conclusion. Instead, the reader is invited to ponder the question posed by the narrative.

YOU SEE, IT'S POSSIBLE TO DELIVER THE WORD OF GOD WITHOUT BEING TRANSFORMED BY THE NATURE OF GOD.

While many ways exist to ask the question implied by Jonah's story, it's best summarized in the question God repeatedly asks Jonah: "Is it right for you to be angry?"

We can empathize with Jonah's dislike for the Assyrians. He thought it'd be just for them to be destroyed. But it's clear that God's goal with this word of judgment was redemption. He wanted mercy. Jonah knew God's nature well enough to know that His word would produce mercy, but he hadn't been transformed by God's nature enough to carry that same mercy. You see, it's possible to deliver the word of God without being transformed by the nature of God.

Ironically, Jonah fails to see how this same mercy leads God to be compassionate with him, to provide him this example with the leafy plant, to almost plead with Jonah to see what He is seeing, and to coach him in His own nature. "Jonah, there are people in there. They don't know what they are doing. Can't you see what I see?"

Jonah was a prophet who delivered God's word but wasn't transformed by God's heart.

He obeyed outwardly, but he couldn't accept God's justice in the form of mercy for people who repented. Jonah ends his story on that hillside, still angry and alone.

Now let's compare the story of Jonah with another prophet—one whose character was quite different.

DANIEL

Daniel was taken as a captive by the Babylonians, the empire that succeeded the Assyrians. He was kidnapped, brought into the royal court because he was healthy and intelligent, and given a Babylonian name. He faced constant tension with remaining faithful to God while living in a foreign empire. In many ways the Book of Daniel is a detailed example of how to be an ambassador of God's kingdom during a wicked empire.

He accepted the Babylonian name but refused to eat any food that violated his covenant with God. With his companions, he proposed a challenge to their overseer. He essentially said, "Let us eat our food and see if we aren't healthier" (Dan. 1:11–13). After Daniel and his friends ate their own food, they were healthier (v. 15).

Later, King Nebuchadnezzar, full of pride, built a giant golden statue of himself and commanded everyone to worship it (Dan. 3:1–5). Daniel's friends—Shadrach, Meshach, and Abednego—refused and were thrown into a fiery furnace. God protected and preserved them (vv. 15–27).

Not long after that act of arrogance, Nebuchadnezzar had a dream that no one could interpret (Dan. 4:4–8). Having successfully interpreted a previous dream, Daniel was brought in to interpret it (v. 25). This new dream, we soon discover, warns that due to Nebuchadnezzar's pride, he'd go mad for a time, and afterward he'd acknowledge God (v. 37).

Daniel is in a similar position to Jonah: delivering a word of judgment to a foreign, wicked king. Look at Daniel 4:19— the moment Daniel is about to deliver this word of judgment to the wicked and prideful King Nebuchadnezzar:

> Then Daniel (also called Belteshazzar) was greatly perplexed for a time, and his thoughts terrified him. So the king said, "Belteshazzar, do not let the dream or its meaning alarm you."
>
> Belteshazzar answered, "My lord, if only the dream applied to your enemies and its meaning to your adversaries!"

Did you catch that?

Daniel didn't gloat. He didn't say, "Ha! Ha! Now you're going to get what you deserve."

Instead, he spoke with humility, essentially saying, "I wish this word were for someone else. I'm sorry to bring you this harsh word."

He delivered this hard word with compassion, with honor—even to a king who had thrown his friends into fire and exiled him from his homeland.

Jonah's story ends with an unresolved argument on a hillside.

Daniel served king after king, interpreting dreams, releasing God's wisdom, and carrying God's kingdom in the heart of a wicked empire.

God is merciful. His word reached the people of Nineveh, even though Jonah didn't do a good job of delivering it, and even though his idea of justice was different from God's. Out of this same mercy, God reached out to Jonah, coaching him in His nature. But Jonah couldn't see Nineveh the way God did.

THE FIVE GOLDEN ARROWS

With the story of these two prophets in mind, I can finally return to those five golden arrows.

After seeing the angel snatch those golden arrows before they could strike my friend, I spent a long time hurt and confused. Had I said something incorrectly? Had I done something wrong? Was something missing in my theology? It wasn't until many years later, after I spent time studying this juxtaposition between Jonah and Daniel, that the Lord finally gave me an answer.

I sat in my office, having read the Book of Jonah for the fiftieth or sixtieth time. I was picturing my friend's angel, pulling the three golden arrows from its chest, adding them to the two in its hand, and placing them in the cupholder of my car. I remembered what the angel said: "I'm sorry, but your arrows are too dirty. You'll have to try again another time."

I remembered the first thought that came to my mind

after the angel left, as I stared at the five arrows in my cupholder: "But they look perfectly clean to me."

Running this through my mind as I sat in my office, I heard the Lord speak.

"My son," He said, His voice full of compassion, "you saw those arrows as you saw them, not as I saw them. You could not see what they were missing. You could not see what was on them. You did not know what you were doing."

I felt a wave of understanding rush through me. As good as my intentions were, as patient as I had been in readying myself for the encounter with my friend, and despite how many years I had spent seeking to be transformed by God's nature, I wasn't releasing gold from God's kingdom. I was launching arrows from my empire to my friend's, and I couldn't tell the difference.

> WHY DO SOME GOOD THINGS FAIL TO PIERCE THROUGH THE VEIL? BECAUSE SOMETIMES WHAT WE THINK IS ROOTED IN GOD'S KINGDOM IS REALLY ROOTED IN OUR OWN.

Why do some good things fail to pierce through the veil? Because sometimes what we think is rooted in God's kingdom is really rooted in our own. Why did my golden arrows fail to pierce my friend? God, in His mercy, was protecting one of His children from the arrows of a foreign empire—my empire.

I sat for several minutes, wrestling with a profound sense of disappointment. My arrows, the statements that they represented, didn't fail to impact my friend because of a minor doctrinal error or a problem with my rhetoric. They failed because of something deeper. Something that, even in this moment of revelation, I was still blind to.

Though I still felt the deep disappointment of this realization, I knew that I had to choose how I'd respond. I could sulk and whine, insisting I had tried my best and my intentions had been good. I could've blamed my friend, convincing myself that if he were more receptive, he would have been able to receive what was good in my arrows, despite whatever was bad. But both would have been little different from Jonah, arguing with God on the hillside, convinced that his own form of justice and righteousness was superior to God's.

Whenever we arrive at a moment where we discover friction between our nature and God's, we have a choice to make: Let God shape us, or let us shape our own idea of God. In the next two chapters, we'll explore why we experience this kind of friction and how we can posture ourselves to engage with God in a productive way. My goal in this moment, when God confronted me about those arrows, was to accept that we've all fallen short of God's glory. But we all need to be taught by Him how to move closer to it—something that Jonah was unable to accept.

I have to be honest. When I listen to the breadth of Christian voices across the world, across social media, and in our churches, I hear far too many that sound more like Jonah than Daniel. Don't get me wrong. Many voices speak and act in a way that reflects the nature of

God. But many others speak truth without carrying the tone of a transformed life.

I hope you don't hear this critique coming from a place of superiority. I'm no better. I have built my own empire and called it God's. I've chosen to incorporate facets of God's kingdom while neglecting others. I've failed to represent God's kingdom, even to one of my closest friends. It's from this place that I urge you to pursue transformation. Study the Bible. Be influenced by spiritual mothers and fathers. Place yourself in a Christian community. Practice abiding in God's presence. Pursue His nature with every fiber of your being. He'll be faithful to reveal Himself to you.

It's not enough to speak the Word of God. We have to speak from the nature of God.

The only way to carry His nature is to be transformed by Him over and over again, especially if we want the opportunity to influence culture the way Daniel did.

CHAPTER 12

THE PROBLEM OF SIN

SEVERAL YEARS AGO, I visited a church in New England. This particular church spent a large portion of its time and resources ministering to the homeless in the area. They had become so successful that the city had given them access to several buildings, as long as they continued their work with the homeless population. When I came to speak at this church, half the group who came to listen were regular church attendees and the other half were homeless people.

One of the first people I met after arriving at the church was a woman I'll call Dolores. Dolores was in her mid-sixties; she didn't have a home, she didn't smell very good, and she wore her wiry gray hair in a short, messy ponytail that stuck right out from the top of her head.

Dolores seemed to have a mental disability. She would switch subjects mid-sentence, weaving in and out of different levels of coherence. She spoke with the volume and tone of a person trying to get the attention of someone on the other side of a crowded room, even if she was standing right in front of you. I'm not trying to be cruel in my description of Dolores; I'm just trying to present her as she was. The truth is, from the moment I met her, I felt a deep sense of affection for her.

Her all-caps tone of voice was surprisingly endearing: "HEY! NICE TO MEETCHA!" Her often rambling and unclear stories were charming: "LOST MY FAYVERT PENNY AT THE GROCERY STORE YESTERDAY." I instantly fell in love with Dolores.

I was speaking for several sessions at the church over a few days, so I had plenty of opportunities to chat with Dolores after each session. Sometimes her commentary was reasonably coherent: "I LIKE THE PART WHERE YOU TALKED ABOUT THAT ANGEL FELLA." Other times it wasn't so clear: "YOU HAVEN'T SEEN MY LAST PENNY, HAVE YOU?"

After one of the afternoon sessions, I sat down to review my notes for the next message I had planned. Dolores walked up to me, as she had after each teaching, and offered her feedback: "I AIN'T TOO SURE 'BOUT WHAT YOU SAYIN', BUT I LIKE THE WAY IT SOUNDS."

"Thank you, Dolores. I appreciate that," I said with a smile on my face.

She stood staring at me for a moment when suddenly her expression took on the greatest sense of lucidity I had seen in her yet. She looked directly into my eyes for the first time and said, "You know, my parents used to beat me when I was a kid."

Thrown off by the sudden coherence in her eyes and the frank sadness of what she had said, I stumbled over my words a little. "I-I'm sorry, Dolores. I'm sorry that happened to you."

"Yeah, they used to beat me so bad sometimes that I couldn't fall asleep at night."

"I'm so sorry, Dolores. That shouldn't have happened to you."

"Yeah, I still cry about it sometimes."

"I'm sorry, Dolores."

The unusual clarity in her blue-gray eyes faded as quickly as it had come, and then she said, "Well, that's OK. Gotta go look for my penny." Then she walked away.

I sat in stunned sorrow for several minutes. Anger and sadness mixed and mingled in the cavern of my chest. Maybe it was the blunt tragedy with which she had said it. Maybe it was because her limited mental faculties made it easy to imagine the kind of child Dolores had been. Whatever the reason, I found myself incapable of getting on top of my feelings.

FLOORED BY A VISION

Amid this mingled sadness and frustration, I saw a vision. I saw two people standing before me: a middle-aged man and woman wearing shabby clothes, with messy hair and semi-vacant expressions. Immediately I knew these were Dolores's parents. Signs of alcoholism were on their faces.

They looked disconnected and uncaring; they looked exactly like the kind of people who would mistreat their child.

Seeing this, my frustration only grew. Of course, millions of people struggle with alcohol abuse. Millions are born into or find themselves in poverty. Many end up in similar circumstances for understandable reasons. Despite this I felt deeply angry at these two people. I could see the cost of their mistreatment in Dolores's life. I could see how much had been stolen from her, and it made me angry.

As I struggled to control this feeling of growing angst, I felt the Lord draw His hand across these two people. Then He asked, "Should I punish them?"

The question, which had been asked in a calm and measured tone, poked a hole in my swelling anger. I was reminded that every parent has failed their children to one degree or another, and that all have sinned and fallen short of the glory of God. But still, the injustice in Dolores's life remained—an injustice that deserved some kind of answer.

Not knowing how best to respond amid my swirling emotions, I gave the classic prophetic cop-out, "I don't know, Lord."

Immediately the vision expanded. Above and behind Dolores's parents, I saw each of their parents, and they looked exactly like the kind of people who would raise a son and daughter who would go on to abuse and mistreat their child. They looked equally grungy and broken.

I felt the Lord draw His hand across this row of four

people who stood above and behind Dolores's parents. "Then should I punish them?"

"I don't know, Lord," I answered again, my sense of sorrow growing.

The vision expanded further. Above and behind each of Dolores's grandparents, I saw each of their parents. Above and behind them, I saw each of their great-grandparents. Then, I saw each of their great-great-grandparents. The pattern continued, growing into a massive, inverted pyramid of people—each generation after generation shaped by cycles of abuse, alcoholism, addiction, and poverty. I could see how each generation had the deck stacked against them, how they were each born into injustice and tragedy. A cascading waterfall of sin poured down the generations, culminating—at least for now—in Dolores.

I felt the Lord draw His hand across this whole image, spanning thousands of years of pain and loss. He asked, "Then who should I punish?"

I watched Dolores amble out of the sanctuary as the vision slowly faded, a feeling of loss weighing down my heart. Despite her limited capacity, it was easy to see the beautiful soul at the center of Dolores's broken life. It was painful to imagine what glory could come from a soul such as hers if it had only been given a better chance.

We've spent much of this book discussing the structures and empires we create—structures that are so often born from that first sin, eating from the tree of the knowledge of good and evil. Sin is any act, thought, or system not aligned with God's nature. Structures and empires that aren't in alignment with the kingdom of

God are founded on sin, which is why human empires will always produce injustice.

Sin isn't just about individual action. Of course, when a person steals, lies, abuses, exploits, or even murders, those sins have consequences for them. But what about the sins done to us? What about the sins we commit as a culture? In that vision I saw thousands of sins. I saw individual sins—people stealing from one another, abusing their spouses and children, lying to escape consequence, and much more—but I also saw the effect of sin on each person. I saw how each mistreatment and abuse hardens hearts, turning the abused into abusers and the cheated into cheaters.

> YOU'VE LIKELY HEARD SIN SUMMARIZED IN THE PHRASE "MISSING THE MARK." BUT IT OFTEN NEGLECTS TO ADDRESS THE QUESTION: "WHAT IS THE MARK?"

This inverted pyramid of people represented generations of culture: an influence passed from mother to son to father to daughter, over and over. Your story and outcome may not be as dramatic as Dolores's, but you were still born into a culture like hers. This waterfall of sin produces person after person who wrestles with addiction and abuse and structures and ways of living that form a culture of sin. Though the outcome is different for each of us, the process is the same: Sin forms culture, and a culture of sin feels normal to those who are born into it.

Sin produces a culture where it's normal to hate or fear someone because of the color of their skin. Sin produces a culture where it's acceptable to view the poor as having low character. Sin produces a culture where it's normal to conduct business in a way that exploits others. It produces a culture where the ends justify the means, where might makes right, where wealth is status, and where selfishness is a virtue.

We weren't made for a world with sin in it. We were made for a garden. We were designed to be cultivators of that garden. Because of sin, our gift of cultivation has been turned toward building empires of our own. We've all been born into families, cultures, and nations birthed by this legacy of sin. How, then, can we hope to transform a culture that has already formed us?

You've likely heard sin summarized in the phrase "missing the mark." This is a helpful simplification of what sin is, derived from the Greek word for sin, *hamartia*. But it often neglects to address the question: "What is the mark?"

The mark is God's nature. The mark is His kingdom.

HOW DO WE BECOME TRANSFORMED?

If we want to transform culture and the world, if we want to transform the world, the only way we can hope to do so is to be transformed ourselves. We must engage in the process presented to us as a challenge in Romans 12:2:

> Do not conform to the pattern of this world, but be transformed by the renewing of your mind. Then you will be able to test and approve what God's will is—his good, pleasing and perfect will.

If we want to know what God's will is, what His nature is, what His kingdom looks like, then our minds need to be renewed. Without such transformation we'll see the same result I experienced when I released those five golden arrows toward my friend. Instead of carrying God's transformational power, I released arrows from one empire to another.

So how do we become transformed? The modern Christan answer sounds something like: "Pray, read your Bible, and go to church." Though I strongly believe in the value of these practices, I'd humbly suggest that these three—alone or together—won't inherently produce a transformed mind or a transformed heart.

As with Jesus' disciples, we're called to follow Him, to be imitators of His nature, and to become like Him. This is the primary call of the Christian life: to follow Jesus. The only way to be truly transformed is to dedicate our lives to Him as disciples of Jesus. He is the perfect representation of God's nature and His kingdom, which is why so many of Jesus' parables speak about what the kingdom of God is like. Through His ministry, His teachings, and His actions, Jesus both modeled and taught the kingdom of God.

What it means to follow Jesus—how to do this every day, how to dedicate our whole lives to becoming more like Him—is a subject that could encompass several books. I can't hope to do this subject justice in the remainder of this book. However, I hope that revealing the core problem—that we are exiles from a garden, living in a world full of empires built on the knowledge of good and evil and operating as ambassadors of God's kingdom on the earth—will inspire you to dedicate your time and energy to truly becoming a disciple. The following is a short list of books that I've found have great inspiration and wisdom on this subject:

- *The Pursuit of God* by A. W. Tozer

  This is a beautiful and poignant exploration of what it means to pursue the presence of God with our whole heart. Tozer's rich language and dedicated heart inspire us to focus on God without letting the distractions of life pull us away.

- *My Utmost for His Highest* by Oswald Chambers

  This classic piece of Christian wisdom is structured as a daily devotional, making it easy to integrate into a daily routine of reflecting on God. It is full of insightful ruminations on the nature of God, Christianity, and following Jesus.

- *Mere Christianity* by C. S. Lewis

  C. S. Lewis is one of my favorite Christian thinkers. His style may be a little dense for some tastes, but the richness of the revelation beneath the text is well worth the effort. This book is much more than an apologetic defense of the faith. It's a heartfelt and detailed exploration of what it means to be a Christian.

- *Practicing the Way* by John Mark Comer

    This is by far the most recent of the books I'm recommending, and therefore it may be the best place to start for anyone who's looking for something written in contemporaneous language and addressing modern issues. I'm a great fan of all Comer's books, but this is his most pointed exploration of what it is to be a disciple of Jesus in the modern world.

I've read each of these books multiple times and strongly recommend that any Christian do the same. However, I encourage you to carry this thought with you: Being a disciple of Jesus isn't about acquiring knowledge. Knowledge will help you see and understand what it is to be a disciple, but knowledge isn't the goal. The goal is to become like Jesus. This isn't something we learn or do, though it is informed by what we learn and evidenced by what we do.

It's like the advice so many of us received when we were young and asked how we could know the right person to marry: "You will know when you know." This is a piece of advice rooted in the same truth. The goal isn't to find a person who matches your list of ideal qualities. The goal is to become the kind of person who can recognize who you want as your partner in life.

Becoming a disciple isn't about learning all the lessons Jesus has to offer and being able to recite them in a list. It's about becoming the kind of person who can recognize the nature of Jesus. We pray so that we spend time quieting our hearts and practicing being in His presence. We read the Bible so we can be familiar with the history of God's relationship to mankind.

We go to church so we can learn from others who are following Jesus and have real-world practice being a disciple in a community of others who are doing the same. None of these practices inherently make us a disciple, and all of them have profound benefit and meaning far beyond what I've listed here, but

BEING A DISCIPLE OF JESUS ISN'T ABOUT ACQUIRING KNOWLEDGE. THE GOAL IS TO BECOME LIKE JESUS.

they give us the opportunity to discover what it means to be a disciple.

Before you set this book down and pick up one of the others I recommended, I have one last story to share with you. I told the first part of this story in my second book, *Profound Good.* However, this story left me with a question not so different from the one I had after my encounter with the five golden arrows.

The answer to that question came to me years later, and with it the most important quality for anyone who wishes to become a disciple of Jesus—a quality Jonah lacked and one many Christians lack today. In my opinion, it's the single most important quality for anyone who wants to be an ambassador of God's kingdom and to avoid building a kingdom of their own.

CHAPTER 13

BEING TRANSFORMED

SEVERAL YEARS AGO, I was speaking at a conference in eastern Texas. I had just finished a long Q and A session when a woman approached me with a reserved posture.

"Excuse me," she said in a quiet voice. "I have one more question, if that's all right."

"Sure thing," I said.

"Well, it's not a question exactly." She rubbed her hands together, her gaze drifting between me and the floor. "Is there any chance you'd be willing to pray for my daughter?"

"Sure, I'd be happy to do that," I said, noticing how nervous she looked.

"OK, great, I'll uh... I'll just go see if she's willing to come into the building."

I hesitated for a moment, running through my mind all the possible reasons her daughter might not want to come into the building. "Sounds great."

Later that evening, the woman approached me again.

"OK, she's willing to come into the building, but she won't come into the sanctuary. Would you be willing to meet with her in the foyer?"

"I suppose that would be fine," I answered, not quite able to keep the confusion out of my tone.

"Maybe I should explain."

"That would be great."

She took in a deep breath and spoke, her voice cracking over the first few words. "We're just a normal church family, you know? But earlier this year, my daughter met this...young man. My husband and I didn't feel great about him, but he seemed nice enough. He kept buying her expensive gifts and being too affectionate. Anytime we tried to talk to our daughter about it, she would get so defensive. It even got to the point where she was sneaking out at night with him. Well, even though we were not too sure about this guy, we were shocked when he kidnapped her and took her into the world of human trafficking."

She paused for a moment, biting her lip as she held back a wave of tears.

"We called the police, of course, but it took them three months to track her down, and she was two states away when they found her." Tears flowed freely down her face as she continued, "It's just been hard, you know? We have her. She's back, but it's just not the same. I mean, how could it be? She's only fifteen." She broke off in another gush of tears.

My arms and legs felt numb. I had been completely silent as she recounted her story, unable to find an adequate response. My heart ached. My mind raced. I kept thinking about my own daughter—about how I felt when she skinned a knee or when someone was mean to her at school. I was afraid to even imagine how I'd feel if anything like this happened to her.

"I can't say how sorry I am," I finally said. "I would be happy to pray for her."

"OK," she said, not bothering to wipe away the tears anymore. "I'll get her."

I felt terrified as I waited in the foyer. I feared doing or saying anything that might make the situation worse than it already was. What could I possibly say that would help? How could I make sure to avoid causing any more pain?

People are sometimes scared when they meet me because they worry that I'll see some horrible demon or spiritual wound on them. Though I see both frequently, they almost never lead me to judgment. The truth is, when you honestly see the pain and the fruits of pain in others, it creates the purest compassion and the deepest empathy.

Imagining the empathetic pain I'd feel seeing what this girl had been through caused some cowardly part of me to want to run out the back door. I was afraid to see her wounds—afraid to feel compassion and empathy for such agony. I knew it wasn't my job to fix her. I knew I couldn't. I knew all I had to do was hear what God had to say, and I knew He'd speak. But still, I was afraid.

Suddenly, the doors burst open. Startled, I completely shut off my ability to see in the spirit as the woman walked in. Her daughter was behind her, and a family friend followed with a tender hand on the young girl's back.

The anxiety rushing through my veins vanished in an instant, replaced by a slow, deep ache. Everything about the girl's expression, posture, and stance screamed of deep anguish. Her eyes darted constantly between the ground, the ceiling, and somewhere in the distance, never meeting mine. She crossed her arms across her chest, fidgeted with her hands, and then shifted the position of her feet with every breath.

A primal empathy welled up in my soul. It was deeper than the empathy of a minister—even deeper than the empathy of a father with a daughter of his own. It came from my very foundation: one human capable of feeling pain recognizing another human feeling deep pain. Every part of me wanted to help, but every part of me didn't know how.

"Here she is," her mother said, trying to sound cheerful.

"All right," I said. "Let's pray."

Wanting to take it slowly, I looked down at the ground and activated my gift, deciding it would be easier if I started with her feet and worked my way up.

I made it to her shoes. Her wounds were so severe that the blood running down her legs was filling both of her gray sneakers. The full force of the empathetic pain I had expected came spiking through me. Every other sensation shut down in the face of such impossible pain. I clenched my eyes shut, unable to handle the sorrow.

My doubts ran through me again. How could I say anything in the face of such pain? How could I do anything but add to her confusion and trauma? Despite these raging doubts, something deeper rose in my chest—a courage that insisted, "If I can release even a drop of God's goodness into this situation, it'll be well worth whatever empathetic pain I may feel and the risk of making a mistake." Before I could doubt or think, I snapped both eyes open and looked directly at her face.

Even as I write this, my breath leaves me at the memory of what I had seen. Despite the empathetic pain that had fired through me and the way her posture and expression spoke of all the trauma she had endured, when I looked at her in the spirit, she was perfect. She was absolutely perfect in every way: No scratch, bruise, or speck of dirt was anywhere on her. She looked as perfect, clean, and pure as my own daughter on the day she was born. Nothing was wrong with her at all.

I realized I was seeing her the way God saw her. Even though this is the second time I'm writing this story down—even though I've shared it dozens of times—I still struggle to share the magnitude of what I saw in that moment. I knew she must have had many spiritual wounds. I could feel every bit of the empathetic pain from what had happened to her. But I could also feel God's goodness being pointed at every part of her life.

It wasn't a goodness that covered up what had happened. The perfectly whole and healthy girl I saw in the spirit, standing in front of me, was not a facade. His goodness was so great that it was more than enough for all her pain and suffering. His goodness was so great that it could handle all that had happened to her and see her as perfect with absolute honesty.

Seeing this, I prayed. I shared what I was seeing to the best of my ability. It blessed her mother and the family friend, but the girl didn't respond. She didn't even show any sign that she could hear me speaking.

I walked away from that experience feeling hollow. I had seen something perhaps more beautiful than anything I had ever seen before. God's goodness was more than enough for such a great tragedy. Yet I didn't feel all that goodness release from my mouth as I prayed for her and described what I saw. Yes, it had encouraged her mother, but the girl had not responded.

MORE THAN ENOUGH

When I share this story, some people suggest I was seeing what lay ahead for this girl: the end of a long healing process. I can understand that healing takes time. However, I believe that if they had seen what I had seen, they wouldn't make that assumption. The evidence of His goodness was there, and that goodness was more than enough. Her pain might not have vanished instantly, but His presence would have been more than enough to comfort her throughout her healing. While His goodness might not have allowed her to skip the healing process, it would have given her the courage and hope to engage in that process.

Despite my best efforts, I had not been able to release all the goodness that was available in that moment.

When I fail—and I do often—I can respond in one of three ways. First, I can puff up. Puffing up looks like blaming others, blaming circumstances, and insisting I didn't cause the poor outcome. Puffing up is rooted in pride and sabotages any chance I may have to learn from my mistakes.

Second, I can shrink back. Shrinking back looks like disproportionately putting the blame on myself, beating myself up, and insisting that my shortcomings caused the bad outcome. Shrinking back is rooted in shame and is just as destructive to growth as pride.

Rather than engage in the first two responses, when I fail—when there is an outcome in my life that I'm not happy with—I try to maintain the posture of an open-hearted learner. An open-hearted learner recognizes that their own shortcomings, the shortcomings of others, and the complexity of our circumstances all contribute to a poor outcome. An open-hearted learner is eager to discover what caused the poor outcome—not because they want to know where to assign blame, but because they are eager to grow.

Though I did my best to express the goodness I saw pouring into that young girl's life, I did not feel everything release. Every time I thought about that moment, I would ask the Lord, "Is there anything I could have said, is there anything I could have done, and is there any adjustment I could have made to release more of Your goodness into that girl's life?" For a while I asked this question every day, then every week, then every month, and then three or four times a year. Every time I heard nothing. Years went by, but still I received no answer.

Not long ago, I went outside to mow my lawn. I like working outside. Much of my work involves sitting at a desk these days, so I relish the opportunity to be both productive and active. I threw on some headphones, cranked up the mower, turned on some music, and started cutting a trail through my yard.

I got about halfway done when the memory of the girl came back into my mind. Just as every time before, I paused and asked the same question:

"Is there anything I could have said, is there anything I could have done, is there any adjustment I could have made to release more of Your goodness into that girl's life?"

Then, quite unexpectedly, I got an answer.

I saw a vision. It was a vision of a young man. Though I had never seen this young man before, I recognized immediately who he was. This was the guy who had kidnapped that fifteen-year-old girl.

I don't consider myself an angry person, but the moment I saw this vision of the young man, my blood began to boil. I have lived long enough and seen in the spirit long enough to know people choose to do bad things for many reasons. As I've said before, I see great value in recognizing the nuance that exists in so much of life. However, no reason I could imagine, no nuance I searched for, could stifle the anger I felt toward this young man.

I couldn't imagine how anyone could be so callous, so cold, as to put a price on a person's innocence. I stared at him in this vision, tearing at his appearance with my thoughts. He looked like the kind of guy who would kidnap a fifteen-year-old girl, with his shifty eyes and disgusting smirk.

In my roiling anger, I felt a familiar sensation as the Lord drew His hand across this young man's chest and asked, "Should I punish him?"

The question felt like a knee to the gut. I had heard this question before. I knew where this vision was going. I thought I knew the point God was getting at. This young man wasn't a singular agent of evil but the product of a legacy of sin—a history that had spanned generations. I should have let the nuance of this truth stay my anger, but it wouldn't.

A deep part of me wanted to answer the Lord's question with a heartfelt "Yes!" But despite my anger, I knew that wasn't the right answer. In truth I still didn't know the right answer. So, as I had before, I gave the only answer that was true:

"I don't know, Lord."

As I expected, the vision expanded. I saw the young man's parents standing above and behind him. They looked like the kind of parents who would raise a son to kidnap and exploit a fifteen-year-old girl. They looked every bit as cold and callous as the young man's actions had been.

As expected, the Lord drew His hand across both the young man's parents. "Should I punish them?"

"I don't know, Lord."

As expected, the vision expanded again. I saw all four of the young man's grandparents, and their parents, and their parents. Once again I watched it build up and up into an inverted pyramid of people. Once again I watched the cascading waterfall of sin pour down from generation to generation—a legacy of exploitation, greed, abuse, and violence.

Then something happened that I didn't expect. The vision expanded once again. At the bottom of this inverted pyramid of people, just under the young man, I saw Jesus nailed to the cross. Generations of sin poured down, sabotaging the life of everyone it touched, stacking the deck against each one, corrupting and twisting, until it landed on Jesus.

THE VISION FADED. I STOOD THERE ON MY LAWN, THE MOWER STILL RUNNING AS I CRIED INTO THE HANDLE. SOMETHING IN HIS GOODNESS AND LOVE HAD ELUDED ME.

In this moment, for the second time in my life, I felt the same goodness that had been present the day I prayed for the girl. Not only had it been enough for all her pain and trauma; it was enough for so much more. Every sin that made up that cascading waterfall, every cause and effect it had throughout the generations, and every consequence and outcome, His goodness was more than enough for it all.

Then I turned and looked at the young man at the bottom of that inverted pyramid, and I saw that this same goodness was pointed directly at him. I wish I could say I was deeply touched in this moment by the revelation of God's nature, but I must be honest. When I saw God's goodness pointed at that young man, my anger flared right back up to the surface.

174

I screamed in the depths of my soul, "Get that away from him! Get that away from him! That doesn't belong to him!" Seeing God's goodness poured out on someone who had done something so cruel and so vile felt deeply wrong. I couldn't reconcile God's goodness pointed at someone like him.

At this point I should remind you: I am a Christian. I know how the gospel works. I know that Jesus died for everyone. Out of obedience to the gospel, I could have stated that it was OK for God's goodness to be released to this young man. But, like Jonah, this would have been a dishonest form of obedience.

It's not enough to be obedient to God's will; we must be transformed by His nature.

Though I knew I was wrong and that God has every right to release His goodness on whomever He chooses, I was still unable to align my feelings with His nature, so I spoke the truth: "God, I don't know how to do that. I don't know how to make allowance for Your goodness to be pointed at someone like him. Not that I have any right to allow You to do anything."

The Lord spoke in a voice both gentle and firm, "Well, that's too bad, because that kind of goodness is the only kind that could have reached that girl in the midst of her pain."

"TEACH ME TO BE LIKE YOU"

The vision of the inverted pyramid of people faded. I stood there on my lawn, the mower still running as I cried into the handle.

I had asked the question hundreds of times: "Is there anything I could have said, is there anything I could have done, is there any adjustment I could have made to release more of Your goodness into that girl's life?" And here was my answer. Because my notion of God's goodness was incomplete, I was unable to express it to the girl completely.

Something in His goodness and love—something I still can't fully define, but something related to His choice to send His Son to die, even for the most wicked of sinners—had eluded me: the ability to love both victim and victimizer. Though I could feel the reality of that love coursing through my veins as I stood there crying into my lawn mower, I couldn't name it then, and I can't name it now.

So I wiped away my tears and told the Lord, "I don't know how to love like this. Will You teach me to become love?"

If we want to be disciples of Jesus, a moment comes that each of us will have to face. We will face it more than once. Sometimes we'll face it more than once in a day. This moment will determine if we've truly decided to be His disciples. It is the moment we discover that friction exists between our nature and His.

When this happens, we have a choice to make: Let God's nature shape ours or let our nature shape His.

We can't change God, of course, so instead of changing His nature, we'll change our idea of His nature, thus building another empire. Instead, when faced with the friction between our nature and His, if we humble ourselves and ask, "Please teach me to be more like You," we will be on the path to becoming a disciple.

I believe the single most valuable quality any disciple of Jesus can have is the ability to recognize the friction between their nature and His—and respond by humbly asking, "Teach me to be like You."

Unfortunately, this isn't the common response. When we read the Bible and find friction between our notion of righteousness and Jesus', we usually look for ways to bend Jesus' words to match our ideas. This is true of many facets of life: from family to our response to the poor, from the treatment of foreigners to our sexual identity, from how we treat our enemies to much, much more.

IF WE WANT TO BE DISCIPLES OF JESUS, A MOMENT COMES THAT EACH OF US WILL HAVE TO FACE. WE WILL FACE IT MORE THAN ONCE.

We must decide if we want our beliefs and values to be shaped by our discipleship to Jesus or by the traditions and empires our fathers and mothers built. I don't know what your beliefs are, but I guarantee that some of them are not coherent with God's nature. Becoming a disciple means giving up your right to the knowledge of good and evil. It means submitting that right to God and following Jesus.

To anyone considering whether they are willing to engage in a journey of this magnitude, I'll offer this one warning: You don't get to choose the consequences of an untransformed life.

My unwillingness to engage in forgiveness toward the

young man who had kidnapped that girl prevented me from releasing God's goodness into her life. My value for my own ideas about righteousness and what it means to follow God meant that, when I tried to share truth with my friend who had abandoned the faith, an angel had to protect him from my attempts to help him. Jonah's hatred of the Assyrians did not bring calamity on the Assyrians; it brought calamity on him.

We don't know what fruit will sprout from the seeds of sin. I don't say this to scare you; I say it because it's the truth. Jesus didn't say, "Sell all you have and follow Me," just to make a point about material possessions. I believe this call applies to all our philosophy, politics, traditions, and values. Give it all up and follow Him. This is what it means to be a disciple. If you can't, then ask yourself, "Why not?" You may find some friction between your nature and His.

God is merciful. Jesus' disciples made so many mistakes in misjudging and misinterpreting His nature. Jesus was faithful to correct and guide them. Jonah experienced tremendous friction between his nature and God's. In the story we saw how kindly and intimately God tried to coach Jonah through this friction. God has been just as kind and merciful with me, and I know He will be with you.

If you look at the world and wonder why so much wickedness exists, it's because we are exiles from a garden, living in a world full of empires built on the knowledge of good and evil. But you should not despair because God sent His Son to be an example of how we can become gardeners again. He paid the impossible debt that sin has imposed on generation after generation. All we need to do is follow Him.

If we want to transform the world, we must be transformed ourselves. If we want to transform ourselves, we must follow Jesus.

CONCLUSION

THE OTHER DAY I was heading to the grocery store to pick up a few things before dinner. I had just pulled into the parking lot when I got an alert on my phone. The Atlanta area was expected to receive an inch of snow in the next two hours.

"I have about fifteen minutes," I thought.

I don't know how it is where you live, but in Georgia, snow is considered grounds for a state of emergency. Traffic turns to gridlock, the bread and milk disappear from the store shelves—you know, end-of-the-world stuff. I grew up near mountains, and my dad had taken me to learn how to drive in the snow the same week I got my learner's permit, so I'm perfectly comfortable driving in snow. But I realize I'm not the only person who lives in my city.

I fought the temptation to abandon my store trip and serve leftovers for dinner. I took a deep breath, grabbed a cart, and walked through the automatic doors.

"Uh-oh," I thought. "They're already here."

People were already wandering the aisles with a package of toilet paper under each arm, rifling through the milk section, and piling stacks of water bottles in precariously full carts. These were the anxious shoppers. The COVID-19 pandemic gave many the opportunity to experience this phenomenon, but in the Atlanta area, whenever even a possibility of snow exists, we experience this all over again.

I've lived in Georgia long enough to have experienced two serious ice storms. Both were trying for this area, which only experiences snow once every few years. Despite how challenging those experiences had been, I found myself suppressing judgmental thoughts as I made my way toward the few ingredients that I needed to finish the dinner I had planned. I knew that if I wasn't in and out within fifteen minutes, I'd be stuck in line for an hour.

I found myself looking in the spirit as I dodged around people with carts full of frozen dinners, paper towels, and other essentials for such an emergency. I saw wafts of sickly blue vapor bursting around people's heads. Like a steam engine working at too high a pressure, their fear management system was overwhelmed, causing these decompressive bursts. I saw a dozen demons hopping across the tops of the grocery store shelves, looking like hungry kids in a candy store.

I turned down the cereal aisle, remembering that we needed some. There I saw a woman in her late sixties. She had four boxes of Cheerios in her cart and was anxiously eyeing the shelf, considering whether she might need a few more. Three bursts of the dark blue steam erupted from her ears and eyes as she stood there, and a demon hopped off the top of a display and landed on her shoulder.

It pressed a hand over one of her ears, catching a burst of steam in its palm. The dark vapor condensed in its hand, forming a kind of gummy blue sap. The demon rubbed its sticky hand all over the woman's face, smearing the blue sap across her skin. A shudder of anxiety ran through her, and she compulsively grabbed another two boxes from the shelf.

I rolled my eyes. We were expected to get only one or two inches of snow—not nearly enough to cause any serious problem. The snow probably wouldn't even stick on the road. Despite the voice of compassion at the back of my mind reminding me that we had experienced serious complications due to snow in the past, my judgmental attitude continued to flare. I thought, "Look at how she's letting fear control her. Look at how she's letting this demon take advantage of her, all over a few inches of snow."

I could feel my internal empire filibustering its code of justice to my soul. I could, rationally, find plenty of wisdom to support my internal ethics: "You should learn how to drive in the snow, so you aren't afraid of it. You should consider that even if we received several inches of snow, you'd still have plenty of time to buy whatever you need. You should have checked the weather report, then you would know it's going to be warm enough to melt all the snow before tomorrow afternoon. You have no real reason to be afraid."

But I'm not a disciple of rationality. I'm not a disciple of my own wisdom. I'm not a disciple of proper preparedness. I am a disciple of Jesus. And I knew that my attitude was not consistent with His nature.

I took in a deep breath, closed my eyes for a moment, and asked the question I often ask when I discover friction between my attitude toward a person and His: "Jesus, how do You see this person?" Then I opened my eyes again.

As soon as I looked at her again, her whole life flashed before my eyes. I saw her as a little girl, singing and dancing at church. I saw her praying alone in her room. I saw her crying over her Bible, overwhelmed by the beauty she found within its pages. I saw her grow up, remaining faithful to the Lord throughout her life. I saw that she had a powerful gift of discernment from a young age. I saw this gift develop her into a powerful prayer warrior. I watched her intercede for her parents, her friends, her children, and her grandchildren. I watched how this gift of discernment gave her insight into God's purposes for people's lives, but I also saw it give a keen awareness of how much can go wrong in a person's life. I saw how this gift—so strong even when she was young—led her to face fear when she was too immature to know how to handle and process it.

I saw how experiences in her life and in the lives of people she cared about gave her a clear understanding of how dangerous life can be. I saw how this deepened her struggle with fear. But I also saw how vigilantly she fought her battle with fear. She contended for confidence and faith. She sought counsel for her anxiety about her children. I saw how, after she got home, she would repent in her prayer room for how she had let fear take hold of her. More than anything, I saw how profoundly the Lord loved her.

He saw every flaw, every victory, and every failing. Even though my compassion for her had already surpassed my judgment, I could feel that His compassion toward her was a thousand times more powerful than mine. He is a mature Father—the most mature Father. He knows His children. He knows the path they've walked. He has fathered billions. He knows the developmental stage every one of us is in. He has already chosen us. He has already accepted us.

I felt a comforting conviction melt away the final remnants of my negative attitude, and I looked at her with new eyes. Though she was still anxiously looking through the rows of cereal, and though the demon was still rubbing the condensed fear in her face, I was now able to see her with the eyes of a mature father. She was still working out her relationship with fear, but now I could see how well she was doing in that ongoing work.

I helped her grab a few more boxes of Cheerios from one of the higher shelves, and then I rushed through the rest of the store to collect the few items I needed for dinner. As I made my way to the checkout lines, I was grateful to see that they hadn't grown too long. I waited in line, laid my items on the belt, and noticed a young woman who was bagging the groceries at the end of my line. She was somewhere in her early twenties, and she had a sad, almost desperate expression on her face.

My eyes locked with hers for less than a second, and once again I found myself drawn into a vision.

I saw her as a young girl, playing in the woods near her parents' house. I saw her laughing with her siblings and eating dinner with her family in the evening. I saw that though she had a loving family, the structure of that love always came with subtle requirements. When those requirements were not met, when mistakes were made, love would leave the room, if only for a moment.

This lapse in love in her family created a hole in the young woman's heart, a longing for unconditional love. Sadly, her experience with her family caused her to expect the same kind of conditional love from God. Though she attended church with her family regularly, the filter her family system had produced prevented her from seeing the true love of God, making the hole in her heart that much wider.

This emptiness caused her to hungrily hunt for the kind of love that every child of God is designed to need. She first sought this out among friends when she started school. She tried to be friends with the popular girls, bending and shifting her personality to better fit into their social groups. But this always left her even more empty.

As she grew, her hunt for love led her to pursue fulfillment in relationships with boys. Again, she shaped herself to better fit into their lives to keep being wanted, but this too left her empty and disappointed. A pattern emerged as she continually shifted her values and personality to try to gain the love she so desperately needed. Each time it ended in a rejection that left her even emptier than before.

I saw that she was now living with her boyfriend, and the dread on her face came from the realization that he was going to break up with her soon. Many experiences with rejection had given her a keen sense of the buildup to this, and she was already feeling the emptiness settling in. Just as it did with the woman in the cereal aisle, a profound realization of God's love for this young woman filled me as I saw all this.

I wanted to say something to her, but as I formed a response to her circumstances, I noticed a problem— everything I could think to say was not consistent with God's love for her. My understanding of what it means to follow Jesus is not compatible with living together before marriage. Anything I thought to say carried this belief in a way that would have come across as cutting or demeaning. Even the gentlest encouragement I formed in my mind held a tinge of judgment.

I'm a disciple of Jesus. There is no condemnation in Christ. I could make arguments about whether she was *in* Christ or whether her life circumstances were coherent with Christ. They probably would have been good arguments, but the disciple in me knew the truth: Something in my concept of following Christ in this area was not coherent with His nature. I couldn't pinpoint the discrepancy, but I felt it as clearly as a splinter in my foot. Anything I could think to say would not carry His nature.

I still hold my values on this subject. I wouldn't recommend that someone live the way she was, but the disciple in me knew that I was experiencing friction between His nature and mine. Being right is not good enough. Having truth is not good enough. I must carry His nature. Anything I said would have been like those five golden arrows I sent toward my friend: an attack from an empire that heaven would be right to defend her from.

Letting the sorrow of the lost opportunity to release God's kingdom settle in my chest, I smiled at her as kindly as I could, gathered my groceries, and carried them to my car.

BEING RIGHT IS NOT GOOD ENOUGH. HAVING TRUTH IS NOT GOOD ENOUGH. I MUST CARRY HIS NATURE.

I could puff up. I could blame her for her immorality, her inability to stick to the code of ethics she had been raised to keep, condemn her parents for their failings, become enraged at the powers and principalities of this age, or bemoan the wickedness of modern culture. But this would have been rooted in pride—a validation of an empire of my own creation.

I could have shrunk back. I could have blamed myself for not being transformed enough, thought of myself as a self-righteous bigot, tried to bend my values to accommodate Christ's mandate to love everyone, spiraled into depression at the discovery of yet another area where I'm not yet like Jesus, or dismissed the experience—numbing myself from the conviction to be an ambassador of His kingdom wherever I go. But this would have been rooted in shame—the building blocks of an empire of resentment, isolation, and compromise.

Instead, I put my groceries in my car, got into the driver's seat, and sat quietly for a moment. I am a disciple of Jesus. I will probably spend the rest of my life wrestling with the friction between my nature and His. I'm grateful for the opportunity to recognize a place where I still need to grow. I won't compromise His values, His compassion, His truth, or His love. I will humbly pursue it.

I waited in silence for a moment and asked the question I have asked a thousand times since I learned why those arrows failed to pierce my friend, saw how my ignorance about God's goodness made me unable to release it to a young girl in so much pain, and studied how Jonah and many others in the Bible failed to be transformed by God's nature. It's a request I make almost every day, and it's a request I suggest you make in your own time with the Lord:

"God, teach me how to become love. Teach me to be like You. Make me a disciple."

A PERSONAL INVITATION FROM THE AUTHOR

GOD LOVES YOU deeply. Every person on this planet was created to live in a garden. We were all born as exiles from that garden, but we don't have to stay that way. Jesus has redeemed us. He is the way back to the garden—not only when we die but here on earth. You can, right now, become a cultivator of that garden, God's kingdom on the earth. This doesn't mean you have to become a pastor or a monk. You can become an ambassador of God's kingdom wherever you are in life. All you need to do is follow Jesus and imitate Him in your family, your work, and with your neighbors.

If you've never invited Jesus into your life or truly

committed yourself to becoming one of His disciples, you can start right now. Like a marriage, the commitment we make to Jesus is just the beginning of this process. If you would like to make that commitment today, you can pray this prayer with me:

> *Lord Jesus, I want to know You as my Savior and Lord. I believe You are the Son of God and that You died for my sins. I believe You rose from the dead and are alive today. Please forgive me for my sins and for the empires I've built in my life. I invite You into my heart and my life. Make me new; reshape my heart and mind. I commit to walking with You, to becoming Your disciple and an ambassador of Your kingdom. In Jesus' name, amen.*

To hear me personally share about what it means to follow Christ, scan the QR code or visit BlakeHealyBooks.com/throughtheveil/resources. I'd be honored to share a few words of encouragement and pray a blessing over you.

If you've prayed this prayer, either for the first time or as a renewed commitment to discipleship, I encourage you to put action to your commitment. Find a community of people who are following Jesus, learn how to study the Bible, and learn from those who do the same. I will again recommend the following books as excellent resources for anyone looking to learn more of what it means to follow Jesus:

- *The Pursuit of God* by A. W. Tozer
- *My Utmost for His Highest* by Oswald Chambers
- *Mere Christianity* by C. S. Lewis
- *Practicing the Way* by John Mark Comer

If you decided to follow Jesus or if this book has blessed you, feel free to contact my publisher at pray4me@charismamedia.com so we can send you some materials that will help you become established in your relationship with the Lord. You are also welcome to visit blakekhealy.com for more resources, teaching, and links to my other books.

NOTES

CHAPTER 8

1. Michael E. Gerber, *The E-Myth Revisited: Why Most Small Businesses Don't Work and What to Do About It* (HarperBusiness, 2004).

ABOUT THE AUTHOR

BLAKE HEALY IS a best-selling author, speaker, and gifted seer who has spent decades sharing his experiences and insights about the spiritual realm. Known for his ability to make the unseen world tangible and accessible, Healy combines his visionary gifts with practical wisdom and biblical teaching. After fifteen years of leadership at Bethel Atlanta, he now focuses on writing, itinerant speaking, and equipping others to encounter God in transformative ways. He lives in Tyrone, Georgia, with his wife and five children.

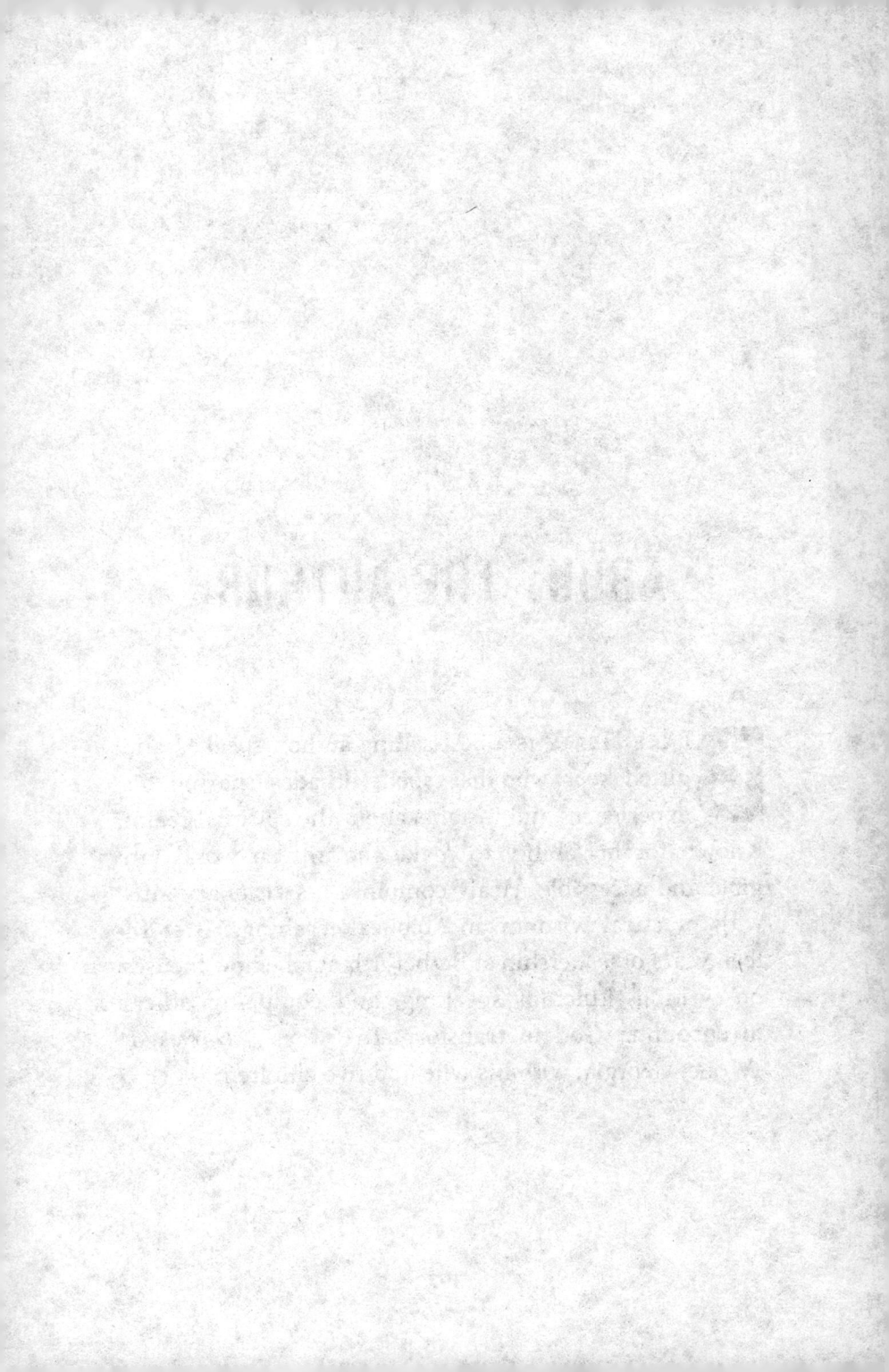